MW00770059

SON OF

CHICKEN QABALAH

SON OF
CHICKEN
QABALAH

Rabbi Lamed Ben Clifford's
(mostly painless)
Practical Qabalah Course

LON MILO DUQUETTE

WEISER BOOKS

This edition first published in 2018 by Weiser Books, an imprint of
Red Wheel/Weiser, LLC
With offices at:
65 Parker Street, Suite 7
Newburyport, MA 01950
www.redwheelweiser.com

Copyright © 2018 by Lon Milo DuQuette
All rights reserved. No part of this publication may be reproduced or transmitted
in any form or by any means, electronic or mechanical, including photocopying,
recording, or by any information storage and retrieval system, without permission
in writing from Red Wheel/Weiser, LLC. Reviewers may quote brief passages.

ISBN: 978-1-57863-615-0
Library of Congress Cataloging-in-Publication Data available upon request.

Cover design by Kathryn Sky-Peck
Interior images by Lon Milo DuQuette
Interior by Steve Amarillo / Urban Design LLC
Typeset in Adobe Minion Pro, Monotype Centaur, Monotype Odense

Printed in Canada
MAR
10 9 8 7 6 5 4 3 2 1

A
NEW
MANUAL
OF QABALISTIC
INITIATION CEREMONIES, TEACHINGS, EXERCISES,
AND PRACTICAL MEDITATIONS CREATED
EXPRESSLY FOR DILETTANTES WITH
REALLY SHORT ATTENTION SPANS
WHO PRETENTIOUSLY CONSIDER
THEMSELVES HERMETIC QABALISTS
BUT WHO, NEVERTHELESS, SINCERELY
DESIRE TO APPLY A TINY PORTION OF THE
HEBREW QABALAH
FOR SPIRITUAL
ENLIGHTEN-
MENT.

DEDICATION

This little book, and everything I mistakenly believe I am; and everything I mistakenly believe I was; and everything I mistakenly believe I shall be; and everything I mistakenly believe I know; and everything I mistakenly believe I desire; and everything I mistakenly believe I love; and everything I mistakenly believe I hate; and everything I mistakenly believe I believe, I mistakenly dedicate
to God/Myself,
who (at the moment) I mistakenly adore as
my Holy Guardian Angel.

CONTENTS

ILLUSTRATIONS AND TABLES

ACKNOWLEDGMENTS

The author wishes to acknowledge the following individuals whose person, presence, or influence is either directly or indirectly responsible for the creation of this work:

Constance Jean DuQuette
(my wife of fifty years)

Donald Weiser and Betty Lundsted
(who first believed in Rabbi Lamed Ben Clifford)

&

Dr. Francis (Israel) Regardie
Paramahansa Yogananda
Dr. Arthur Rosengarten
Dr. David Shoemaker
Robert Anton Wilson
Christopher S. Hyatt
Dr. Timothy Leary
Marc E. DuQuette
Thomas Caldwell
William Heidrick
Charles D. Harris
Aleister Crowley
Paul Foster Case
Dr. I. Z. Gilford
William Breeze
Phyllis Seckler
Carolyn Tillie
Poke Runyon
Chris Chang
Alan Moore
Alan Watts
Rumi

&

to the "Friends and Comrades" of Heru-ra ha Lodge O.T.O.'s Monday Night Magick Class,
who, since 1978, have gathered each week in our living room to take tea and teach me.
You are Our Holy Order or ZIPY or . . .
whatever you want to call it!

You're all Chicken Qabalists!
And I love you!

Author's Notes

The author wishes to remind the reader that the foundational texts of the traditional Hebrew Qabalah are very old. Even the most ancient manuscripts are copies of copies of orally transmitted teachings. Scholars unanimously agree that even the most venerable works are fragmented and corrupted.

Nonsecular Qabalists of the nineteenth century (particularly the scholars and adepts of the Hermetic Order of the Golden Dawn) readily saw what they perceived to be palpable flaws in basic hermetic logic in the manner that fragments of some of the conflicting texts were pieced together. To their hermetically trained eyes, it was obvious where basic repairs could and should be made within various extant versions of the primary texts, especially *The Sepher Yetzirah:[1] A Book on Creation.[2]* The Golden Dawn adjustments are, for the most part, evident and necessary corrections and conform with a thousand years of hermetic thought (including astrological and alchemical systems). They mercifully allow the student to initially embark upon the Qabalistic seas with a few recognizable and comforting landmarks still on the horizon.

A Golden Dawn Qabalah workbook was eventually annotated and published by Aleister Crowley as *Liber 777.[3]* It is a massive collection of tables of Qabalistic correspondences that organizes the Qabalistic, magical, and mythological universe in conformity with the newly adjusted *Sepher Yetzirah*. Rabbi Lamed Ben Clifford used *Liber 777* and the Golden Dawn version of correspondences for his teachings and required his students to own a copy and refer often to it.

However, while he was happy to initially teach the fundamentals of Qabalah by using the Golden Dawn and 777 correspondences, Ben Clifford refused to dogmatically endorse them (or indeed any particular system or textbook, modern or ancient) or ever suggest that one was doctrinally correct, authoritative, or even superior to another. It was clear from his private drawings of the Tree of Life (not included in this volume) that even Ben Clifford deviated in places from the GD-777 correspondences. In fact, once his students had mastered the preliminary degrees of study, he urged them to explore other systems and other ways of looking at everything. As he once wrote to San Francisco socialite and patroness Thalassa Therese:[4]

> Truth is bigger than systems. If you can't uncover truth
> in a flawed system you won't be able to uncover it in a
> perfect one. All are correct! And all are wrong! Don't

worry about it! Learn one, and get comfortable with it. When you are fluent in that system then you will be able to appreciate the nuances and wonders of the others. Just be consistent with the system you are working *while you are working with it*. Don't expect multiple systems to properly support each other; and for heaven's sake don't write me and expect me to validate *any* of your amazing revelations! I hate that s__t!

PROLOGUE

CONFESSION OF A
PSEUDEPIGRAPHIC BIOGRAPHER

By Lon Milo DuQuette

*For a long time we have known that literary forgeries
represent a flight into anonymity and pseudonymity just as
often as they indicate trickery; and not for nothing have we
retained the foreign word, "pseudepigrapha" to designate
in particular a legitimate category of religious literature
. . . the Zohar is the most important but by far not the only
example of such love of masquerade in Jewish literature.*

—Gershom G. Scholem
*Zohar: The Book of Splendor:
Basic Readings from the Kabbalah*[1]

WARNING: THIS BOOK IS
CHICKEN QABALAH VOL II.

I wish to be completely candid by stating at the outset that this book
represents, for all intents and purposes, the *second* volume in *The Chicken
Qabalah of Rabbi Lamed Ben Clifford* series.[2]

This is not to say that this book cannot be read, studied, consumed,
digested, and enjoyed as a self-contained, stand-alone work in its own
right; but I would not be altogether honest if I did not stress the fact that I
wrote and organized it assuming the reader has already read *The Chicken
Qabalah* and is at least generally familiar with the elementary Qabalistic
principles inculcated in that work. The two works were written to comple-
ment and complete each other, and it is my hope that every reader of this
work will place a copy of *The Chicken Qabalah* close at hand as he or she
studies this work.

When I first pitched the idea for the book that would become *The
Chicken Qabalah of Rabbi Lamed Ben Clifford* to my publisher, Donald
Weiser, he appeared to immediately grasp the overall concept of my unorthodox vision and chuckled (in a patronizingly polite way). As he continued
to thumb through my silly pitch-book, his smile broadened a bit more, and

then he said, "Yes, we'll do it. Looks like fun. But we can't be perpetrating a hoax. You'll have to tell them somewhere that *you* wrote it."

I promised I would.

Well . . . here I am again. Sadly, Donald passed away just a few months ago[3] and didn't get the chance to see the newest installment of the Rabbi Lamed Ben Clifford odyssey. However (because I know Donald is still with us somewhere), I'm going to respect his memory and his wishes by again confessing . . . I wrote this book!

I will also confess that this work did not spring from my skull fully formed like Minerva. It actually developed from a series of twelve all-day Qabalah workshops I facilitated over a one-year period in Beijing, China, in the spring, summer, fall, and winter of 2016.

Throughout that busy year, I returned to Beijing every ninety days, at the equinoxes and solstices, and with the help of Ms. Chris Chang (my initiate sister, friend, interpreter, and "Worthy Guide") initiated twelve candidates into the three degrees of an informal Qabalah initiatory "Order," created exclusively for my Chinese students. It was for me the magical and spiritual experience of a lifetime.

The challenge of having to think carefully (always difficult for me) and thoughtfully choose my words for translation was daunting, but it also forced me to reduce each concept to its most unambiguous essence and relate it to the most universal and simple common denominator. I used hundreds of color slides and illustrations, which helped overcome many of the language challenges. Unfortunately, for the purposes of this book, we will have to satisfy ourselves with the written descriptions of many of these.

Each Initiation Ceremony was followed by two days of workshops, exercises, and meditations, all specifically focused on "mysteries," of each degree—in this case, the mysteries are those of the Three Mother, Seven Double, and Twelve Mother Letters of the Hebrew alphabet.

At first, it seemed to me to be the easiest and fastest way to painlessly attune the participants to the Hebrew alphabet and, at the same time, immerse them in the fundamentals of Practical Qabalah. By summer of 2016, I began to see that my informal initiation program had become something more than a lecture and workshop series. I started to seriously organize my material with an eye toward the more substantial and (hopefully) more enduring work you hold in your hands.

So, perhaps I should also confess that the subtitle should probably be

The Secret Initiation Ceremonies, Exercises, and Meditations of a

(not-so-completely fictitious)

Qabalah Initiatory Society

INTRODUCTION

By Lon Milo DuQuette

It has been seventeen years since the release of *The Chicken Qabalah of Rabbi Lamed Ben Clifford*,[1] and twenty-one years since the unexplained disappearance of the controversial "rabbi" whose unorthodox teachings formed the substance of the text. I was initially flattered when asked by my publisher and colleagues to collect and curate the material for what would become that landmark publication. I never dreamed, however, the assignment would become so challenging or so exasperating.

Rabbi Lamed Ben Clifford (his real name is still unknown) was a highly eccentric character.[2] His followers, although few in number, enthusiastically embraced his nonsectarian doctrines and methods. Unfortunately for his biographers (and future students), he rarely committed any of his discourses to writing.[3] He was hopelessly undisciplined and relied almost exclusively upon person-to-person tutoring and informal interactions within a small circle of disciples, *a few* of whom took excellent notes; *most* of whom did not.

After his (still-unsolved) disappearance in July of 1997, his colleagues were burdened with the ponderous task of sifting through the stacks of scrapbooks and manuscripts that towered floor to ceiling in every room of his otherwise charming Long Island beach house. Directing the labor of collating and cataloging was Ben Clifford's administrator (and "magical son") Dr. Gizmo Ben Lamed. I prevailed upon this saintly and good-humored gentleman to be project editor on *The Chicken Qabalah*.[4]

I'm embarrassed to admit that the popularity of *The Chicken Qabalah* came as a complete shock to all of us. From the first week of its release, critics of esoteric literature reacted with extraordinary kindness. Sales figures for *CQ* (while modest compared to those of sadistic erotic novels or gluten-free cookbooks) continue to tolerably satisfy the publisher, who for the last ten years, has urged me to write a sequel. Year after year I declined, arguing one cannot get blood from a turnip. There were simply no more Rabbi Lamed Ben Clifford texts to publish. I was secure in my belief that the material available to us when we researched *The Chicken Qabalah* represented nearly all of the writings, notes, and interviews known at the time to exist.

Happily, that is no longer the case.

RABBI LAMED BEN CLIFFORD—DEAD AT LAST

The story of how all this "new" material came to light is as curious as everything else surrounding the bizarre life of this enigmatic holy man.

Because his disappearance was unexplained and a body was never recovered, Ben Clifford's estate languished in limbo for many years. Legal disposition of his affairs was postponed a dozen times, triggered by "rabbi sightings" reported from around the world. Many of these were obvious hoaxes perpetrated by grief-maddened Chicken Qabalists. Others were disturbingly bizarre and seemed eerily genuine. To this day, many remain unexplained.

Perhaps the most dramatic sighting was bolstered by the testimony of Sister Gina Martini and eleven Carmelite nuns in Albany, New York, who, in 1999, reported being startled after vespers by a partially clad intruder matching the rabbi's description, friskily darting in and out of rows of drying laundry in the convent courtyard. Two years later, police in Orlando, Florida, responded to a disturbance inside the *Noah's Ark* attraction at the *Holy Land Experience* amusement park. A man who boldly identified himself as Rabbi Lamed Ben Clifford was subdued and briefly detained for loudly berating a teenage actor portraying the High Priest Caiaphas and for making lewd comments to the morbidly obese actress portraying Noah's wife.

Naturally, each reported sighting had to be followed up by insurance company detectives whose investigations necessitated repeated postponements of legal proceedings. Finally, on April 1, 2015, Rabbi Lamed Ben Clifford was at last pronounced "legally dead" by Judge Terrence Stool of the Superior Court of Suffolk County, New York. News of the final disposition stirred little interest in the esoteric community—most of whom, like me, were certain *The Chicken Qabalah* would remain the final published exposition of the teachings of Rabbi Lamed Ben Clifford.

Then, on the evening of April 30, 2015, I received a text message from Dr. Ben Lamed:

> OMG! 3 bags full of LBC goodies found @ BNL. pls call
> asap. Apparently ZIPPY real!!! Gizmo.

I immediately phoned Dr. Ben Lamed, who was so excited I could hardly follow the particulars of his rambling narrative. I will attempt to summarize:

Shortly after Judge Stool pronounced Rabbi Ben Clifford legally dead, he discovered a bag of still-warm onion bagels on the sunroof of his car in the courthouse parking garage. Inside the bag, he found an envelope containing a tiny key, along with a handwritten note that read as follows:

> Dear Judge . . . or whoever declared me legally dead.

Hello from the other side!

Don't freak out . . . nobody really dies. But you'll find that out. Just don't worry about it.

I hope you enjoy the bagels, but please don't eat the key. It unlocks storage locker #528 in the kitchen of the cafeteria at Brookhaven National Laboratories here on Long Island.

Take the bagels home, but please deliver the key along with this note to my old friend Dr. Gizmo Ben Lamed at 3520 Greenbrier Rd. in Montauk and direct him to immediately take possession of the contents of the locker. The contents are really, REALLY cool, interesting and important.

I would write more but . . . I'm dead and I keep getting ectoplasm all over the typewriter.

Thanks, and have a nice eternity.

(signed)

"The Late" Rabbi Lamed Ben Clifford

It wasn't easy for Dr. Ben Lamed to gain security clearance to the highly secretive Brookhaven National Laboratories (itself the subject of conspiracy theories concerning the Philadelphia experiment, time travel, and extraterrestrial intercourse). It seems the rabbi's only connection to Brookhaven had been with its one-time director, Dr. Zaia Youkhanna, an Aramaic scholar and amateur Qabalist, who had organized the rabbi's 1975 lecture tour in Baghdad. When Gizmo finally was allowed access to the kitchen area and opened locker #528, he discovered two large and curiously decorated carpets rolled up and propped in one corner. He also found three black plastic trash bags stuffed with documents, notebooks, ritual scripts, a Canadian Army first-aid kit, a pitch pipe, some colored pipe cleaners, and a 1967 *Minimoog* synthesizer.

Gizmo pleaded with me to join him in Montauk, and I immediately cleared my schedule and booked a flight to New York. What we discovered revealed an exciting and previously unknown facet of Rabbi Lamed Ben Clifford's life and teaching methods. The most stunning revelation confirmed the existence of an "Order" resembling the rabbi's alleged Qabalah school, the *Zerubbabel Institute of Philosophical Youth* (Z∴I∴P∴Y∴). Biographers, myself included, had long assumed Z∴I∴P∴Y∴ was purely mythological—a whimsical fable he invented as a teaching device.

It appears we were wrong. The documents revealed that, for a number of years, Ben Clifford was the hierophantic director of a strange and highly unorthodox Qabalistic initiatory society. He didn't refer to it specifically as Z∴I∴P∴Y∴ but rather by the generic designation "Our Holy Order" (O∴H∴O∴).

Passports and unsent postcards confirmed that, beginning in 1984 and continuing every other year, he would disappear for as long as six weeks at a time. Not even his closest Montauk colleagues knew where he went or what he was up to. His Long Island students fantasized he was moonlighting as a spy, or that perhaps he had mistresses. Most of them simply assumed he needed to periodically check himself in for drug or alcohol detox.

In actuality, he was traveling—all over the world—Wales, Norway, Macedonia, Poland, Germany, Australia, Japan, Croatia, Shanghai, Beijing, and Bethel, Connecticut. These were not lecture tours. He traveled to initiate student-candidates into a three-degree Qabalah Mystery School.

The documents discovered in the kitchen locker contained complete scripts for each of the three initiation ceremonies, along with portfolios of degree-specific study materials, toys, exercises, and meditations. For the Chicken Qabalist (or indeed anyone searching for practical applications of Qabalah as a self-transformational practice), these documents are pure gold. It is this material, including scripts and commentaries of the initiation ceremonies themselves, that make up the major portion of this book, which I've tried to order in an approachable format.

I have not been able to determine with any degree of certainty whether or not any of these O∴H∴O∴ "lodges" continue to operate.[5] But, because I am certain that it was the rabbi's wish that his "secret" initiations and exercises be made public after his death, it is clear to me it was his intention that the work of initiating and instructing new members should continue. I have, therefore, organized this book in a format that I believe the good rabbi envisioned—a practical handbook or guide for both the solitary "Chicken Qabalist" and all other adventurous individuals who believe they can play well with others to experience the initiation ceremonies and degree exercises of the O∴H∴O∴ or Z∴I∴P∴Y∴ or whatever you want to call it.

To paraphrase the immortal Rabbi Lamed Ben Clifford: *"Call it anything you want! Don't worry about it! You're a Chicken Qabalist!"*

QABALAH INITIATION:
THE METHOD TO THE MADNESS

By Lon Milo DuQuette

It is the great paradox of Qabalah that study and practice are truly valuable only when you are already thinking like God.

Wake up first! Then study!

—Rabbi Lamed Ben Clifford
from the First-Degree Lecture

The preceding quote is from the *Lecture* section of Rabbi Lamed Ben Clifford's First-Degree Initiation Ceremony. It succinctly summarizes the *raison d'être* of his Qabalah initiation program. Ben Clifford observed that ancient techniques and materials used by religious or traditional Qabalah study programs (while being brilliant and profound for those who have already developed a significant degree of illumination) remain overwhelmingly complex and intimidating to all others who are less illuminated and still striving for that illumination.

The emphasis of Ben Clifford's work at this level was not so much a matter of "educating the unawakened student," but of "awakening the student to be educated." The idea was to trigger the process by putting the student through a series of artfully designed emotional-psychological experiences that essentially mutate the individual on a subconscious level—a process known as *initiation*.

"Qabalah Initiation is not a 'learning' process, but a 'birthing' process," the rabbi once wrote to Irish rock star and critic Rodney Orpheus. "It is as though I am dreaming I am a soul who takes a magic pill that makes me pregnant. And my baby, when it is born, is *me*—the awakened me!"[1]

Initiation is nothing new to the Western mystery school traditions. Indeed, it seems to be the very essence of the process employed by the Egyptian and Greek mystery schools and cults going even further back into pre-history.

A LADDER?

The great modern initiatory societies of the eighteenth, nineteenth, and twentieth centuries, including Freemasonry, Martinists, the Golden Dawn, and the A∴A∴, generally viewed this progressive series of awakenings as an ascent up the ten *Sephiroth*[2] (or Emanations) on the familiar Qabalistic schema, *The Tree of Life*.[3] Rabbi Ben Clifford often referred to the diagram as "a roadmap from godhead to your head."

The Tree of Life graphically illuminates the fundamental Qabalistic doctrines first revealed in the *Sepher Yetzirah*[4] (arguably the oldest and most venerable Qabalistic text). The rabbi's own fanciful "translation" of key sections of the text appears in the *Chicken Qabalah*.[5] In the opening words it reveals that

> Deity . . . created the Universe (with the help of three
> imaginary friends, "Numbers, Letters, & Words") in
> Thirty-Two Mysterious Paths of Wisdom. They consist of
> Ten Sephiroth out of nothing and of Twenty-Two Letters.[6]

The "Numbers" are described as the path of a lightning flash that strikes down from the pure consciousness of godhead (*Sephirah One—Kether, the "Crown"*) through decaying levels of consciousness (*Sephiroth Two through Nine*), until coming to cosmic full stop at the lowest material level of unawakened humanity (*Sephirah Ten—Malkuth, the "Kingdom"*).

While the great initiatory societies of the past did not realistically expect their members to immediately achieve the progressively higher levels of consciousness exemplified by each Sephirah, several prominent initiatory orders designed their dramatic graduated degree experiences as allegorical steps that ascend up the Tree of Life (from Malkuth to Kether). They organized the structure of their initiations accordingly.

The "Twenty-Two Letters" mentioned in the *Sepher Yetzirah* are those of the sacred Hebrew alphabet. They represent the fundamental scaffolding of existence itself. When projected on the Tree of Life, the letters represent twenty-two highly specialized facets of *intelligence* that serve as conduits between the Sephiroth and (like electrical transformers) step up or step down the frequencies of consciousness of the Sephiroth they connect.

While Ben Clifford acknowledged the genius of using the Tree of Life as a model for a series of mystical initiation ceremonies, for his Order he took a much more fundamental (and perhaps more elegant) approach to initiation.

He began with the profound assumption that because the true, unadulterated consciousness of each human is ultimately *godhead*, then godhead already *is* our true, natural, and essential identity. We don't need to *climb* anywhere. Each of us already is number One on the Tree of Life. All lower (sleepier) levels of consciousness with which we may currently identify are illusionary—dream selves that we temporarily *misidentify* as our Self.

According to Ben Clifford, our initial initiatory journey toward enlightenment is not a *tree-climbing* exercise, but instead, a simple process of *remembering, reconnecting, re-attuning,* and *reresonating* with the primal patterns of who and what we already are. Ben Clifford attempted to illustrate this in his "Tuning Fork of God" parable:[7]

> For a moment, let's think of the Supreme Consciousness of Godhead as an infinitely loud musical note (let's say . . . "A"). This supreme "A" note is the *vibration* made by an infinitely huge *mega-A* tuning fork that is the source vibration of God's pure and absolute consciousness. Now, you and I, because we are . . . *made in the image of God,* are also this divine "A" note. Only *we* express it individually, as if we had our own *mini-A* tuning fork.
>
> Our true identity is the *note* (not the tuning fork). When we are fully awake, our personal, private "mini-A" tuning fork is all clean and shiny, and it vibrates in perfect sympathy and perfect unison with God's great universal "mega-A," which sets it to eternally vibrating.
>
> But, in our unawakened dream state, our personal, miniature tuning fork is *not* clean and shiny. It is rusted over by layer upon layer of dreams. With each built-up layer of dream rust, our mini tuning fork loses more and more of its true tone and perfect pitch. With each layer of rust, we fall deeper and deeper asleep to our true identity.
>
> We could attempt to remove the rust from the outside— by trying to chip away, bit by bit, each layer of dream-rust from our personal tuning forks. Indeed, that is exactly what our fellow Qabalists have attempted to do for centuries, by using the hammer of intellect and the dull chisel of their dogma-restricted imaginations. This is really hard work, especially when we consider the fact that the "workman" doing all this chiseling is still asleep—dreaming within layers of dreams far removed from the wise supervision of Godhead.
>
> Our process is different. Like King Solomon (who, when beginning the task of building the house of God,

first entered into the "presence of God" seeking only for Wisdom), we begin by allowing God's big tuning fork to do the hard work for us. We remove the rust by first triggering the primal vibration deep within our little rusted tuning fork, encouraging it to vibrate again in sympathy with the great mega-note—the great *genetic code* of God.

We do this by persistent exposure to formulae of the universal mega-note itself, until our tuning fork can no longer remain unresponsive to its true vibratory nature; until it answers the call and irresistibly begins to quiver and vibrate in perfect sympathy with God's great universal note—until the vibration becomes so intense and pure that every speck of dream rust, every veil of illusion, is buzzed off the surface of our tuning fork and shed from our soul.

What is the "Genetic Code of God"? What are the "formulae of the universal mega-note" whose exposure is going to set our little tuning forks a-tingling?

You, my dear little tuning fork, are the formula; you and the twenty-two letters of the Hebrew alphabet are the code.

The twenty-two letters are alive and are the secret ingredients of a magic pill that, once swallowed, implants itself in the womb of your soul and makes you pregnant with the baby of your own awakened self.

THE GENETIC CODE OF GODHEAD

In a letter written in 1984 to hedge-fund manager Jonathan Taylor, Ben Clifford wrote

Dear Jonathan,

You have written and told me you wish to be "'initiated' into the mysteries of Qabalah."

Let me respond by saying I cannot do that. Only *you* can initiate yourself into the mysteries of Qabalah. However, all the tools necessary to do this are already in your hands.

The twenty-two letters of the Hebrew alphabet (and the mechanics of consciousness they represent) are the genetic code of godhead. If you were fully awake you would see this marvelous code working blissfully away like the components of a well-oiled machine of consciousness. Obviously, you are not fully awake (otherwise you would not be mistakenly believing we are having this conversation), but the code is still hard at work at the heart of your existence, and if you really want to, you can re-attune and re-calibrate yourself to it.

If you really want to be "initiated" into the mysteries of Qabalah, I advise you to immediately take steps to upgrade your hardware, and reboot the *operating system* of your body and mind by forming healthy living habits. At the same time, you will need to consciously and willfully reprogram the *software* of your soul. Repair the dented and raggedy DNA of your slumbering soul by vaccinating yourself with injections of the pure genetic code of godhead. Allow the code to crystalize itself in your blood. Once you are properly inoculated, the code will incubate, replicate, and grow. Eventually, the old you will mutate and become a new, more-awake you. Go then, my son! Go forth and resonate, vibrate, and harmonize with purity of the code. Allow its perfect melody to retune your laughably out-of-tune instrument.

LMD

As the Hebrew alphabet was created in three stages, so, too, the rabbi's initiatory order was composed of three main degrees that exemplify in their turn the powers of the *Three Mother Letters*, the *Seven Double Letters*, and the *Twelve Simple Letters*. These groups of letters are the formulae and patterns of the perfect DNA of Being. I have organized the material to reflect the work of these three degrees and will include

- A brief introduction concerning the Degree Initiation Ceremony.

- A full text of the ritual officers' script of the Degree Initiation Ceremony itself, including notes for costuming, staging, audio, and visual effects. The serious student is encouraged to repeatedly relive these rituals as meditations, solo rituals, or even as group ceremonies.

- A portfolio of study materials including degree-specific exercises, meditations, readings, and ritual observances appropriate to the degree.

And now it pleases me to present to you *Son of Chicken Qabalah: Rabbi Lamed Ben Clifford's (mostly painless) Qabalah Course*. Enjoy it and apply the experience however best suits your spiritual needs and intentions. If, however, you believe you are serious about using the tools of Qabalah to effect fundamental changes in your consciousness; if you believe you are serious about waking up (even a step or two); then I invite you to enter into the rabbi's world and swallow his magic pill, and for the next nine months,[8] consider yourself a "Friend and Comrade"—an initiate of Rabbi Lamed Ben Clifford's (*probably completely fictitious*) Qabalah School. You just might give birth to a new, more awakened *you*.

THE DEGREE CEREMONIES:
INTRODUCTORY WORDS

By Lon Milo DuQuette

Dear Friend and Comrade,

I hate organized clubs, cults, and anything that smacks of profit motivation and hierarchical ego trips. If we're going to do this in your city, here's how it's got to be:

We exist as an initiatory entity only for the hours of the Degree ceremonies themselves. There shall be: No Dues. No Fees. No Oaths of Obedience. No Loyalty Oaths. No Oaths of Secrecy. No Tests. No Exams. No Business Meetings. No Newsletters. No Gossip. No B.S.!

The officers for the initiation ceremonies are: you, me, and a musician/technician (to play a few organ notes and run a simple slide show).

Be prepared to personally shoulder all financial responsibility. (You may, however, graciously accept voluntary assistance in any form.)

I'll send you the scripts and materials.

You book my flights, the hotel, and make all arrangements . . . then . . .

Don't Worry About It!

See you in March.

LMD

—Carbon copy of undated letter to a local organizer

"INITIATION IS NOT INSTRUCTION!" These blunt words were scrawled in the rabbi's unmistakably poor handwriting on the cover page of his own copy of the First-Degree Initiation script. They should serve to remind us that Qabalistic "initiation" is not the same thing as Qabalistic "study" or Qabalistic "practice." This is an important fact to remember, because Ben Clifford's initiatory program was designed not as a classroom course of instruction (that reiterates seven centuries of corrupted manuscripts), but rather as a dramatic, interactive experiential process designed to program fundamental modifications deep in the candidate's psyche[1]—changes that can only be made at deeper levels of consciousness than the cognizant instruments of reason and intellect can reach.[2]

In a scathing letter to the editor of *Yad Magazine* in 1988, Ben Clifford wrote

> God consciousness is the cosmic birthright of every monad of existence. It is *not* reserved only for those who have time to play all day with numbers and Bible verses so they can demonstrate how everything in the universe is probably really something else!

> We proclaim with smug confidence that the Hebrew alphabet (with its Three Mother Letters, Seven Double Letters, and Twelve Simple Letters) is the formula and blueprint of being and existence itself. But are we so arrogant as to believe that anyone who cannot speak a certain language or learn a certain alphabet is barred from activating and accessing the universal formulae these letters symbolize?

> Hell, no! I'm a Chicken Qabalist![3] Even if the Hebrew alphabet never existed . . .

> - 3 would exist!
>   - » Space-Time would still be a phenomenon of a threefold environment of *Up/Down; Right/Left; Front/Back.*
>
> - 7 would exist!
>   - » There would still be an *Above* and a *Below*; an *East* and a *West*; a *North* and a *South* all surrounding a *Center* point. *Light* and *Sound* would still fracture and organize in sevenfold primary spectrums of color and music.

- 12 would exist!
  - » The six directions would still intersect at twelve oblique angles. Light and Sound would continue to fracture and organize as twelvefold secondary spectrums of color and music.

  Even if we could not read or write or add or subtract numbers, the sacred alphabet would still be creating and holding existence together, still penetrating our souls as color vibrations that excite the cones and rods of our eyes; still be resonating in our ears as the ordered harmonics of the music of the spheres.

  As Qabalists, we must first swallow these primordial seeds and plant them deep in the secret center of the soul; then let them germinate quietly inside us, as we tinker with numbers and plod along with what we think is our Qabalistic studies.

  Look! You can memorize and juggle and manipulate the numbers and Hebrew letters and words till kingdom come! You can dissect the scriptures till your beard reaches your knees. But if you haven't first inseminated yourself with the pure, innocent, fundamental code, your seeds will be defective, and you will only succeed in making yourself pregnant with a Qabalistic monster—an altogether unpleasant bore of an individual, obsessed with your own infinite and irrelevant Qabalistic *revelations*—connecting everything in the universe to everything else . . . but *yourself*!

Following the classic format of the *Egyptian Book of the Dead*,[4] Ben Clifford's degree ceremonies follow the exploits of the awakening candidate as he or she unfolds from one level of consciousness to another. At each step, the candidate is met with resistance that is overcome by a peculiar character-building adventure that involves surviving an ordeal specifically linked to the dynamics of the degree.[5] Passing each degree's ordeal literally mutates the candidate's consciousness so that he or she becomes a new conscious entity, freshly equipped to perceive and function at the new level, and capable of absorbing that level's new lessons and mysteries.

Degree-specific secret words, gestures, grips, and other seemingly silly claptrap and signs of recognition are an important aspect to the initiation experience. During the course of the ceremony, they are repeatedly drilled into the candidate, until they become as familiar as a song. There is a very good reason for this. The ceremonies are designed to trigger subsequent and more intimate initiatory dreams and visions in which the candidate must make use of the Signs, Grips, and Words as tools to resolve more personal (and often more terrifying) metaphoric challenges.

Hotel Temple of Initiation

It is clear by the notes that accompanied the scripts that most of the initiation weekends were held at hotel venues, the *Temple* and *waiting area* being a private banquet room and adjacent conference room. Officers and candidates were lodged for the weekend at the same hotel and able to conveniently rest and refresh themselves during breaks.

The First-Degree ceremony was ideally conferred upon three candidates per occasion. It focused on the mysteries of the dawn of consciousness and the birth of the Three Mother Letters of the Hebrew alphabet. It was a lengthy ceremony, breaking late in the afternoon for a formal dinner and then a rest period, before continuing late in the evening.

The Second- and Third-Degree ceremonies were obviously designed to be conferred upon one candidate at a time.[6] The Third-Degree ceremony was also lengthy and included a formal dinner and rest period, followed by a "Midnight Meditation." Other Third-Degree Initiates living in the vicinity were invited to attend the dinner and meditation, and it appears that it was always an occasion for the warm fellowship such as one might expect from any fraternal organization.

As much as possible, I have reproduced the scripts of the three degree initiations exactly as Dr. Ben Lamed and I found them. I have tried to clearly delineate my editor's comments in footnotes or in other bracketed notes within the text.

FIRST-DEGREE
Preliminary Notes

This version of the script is written assuming the Candidate is female.[1] Those wishing to perform or exemplify the ritual may easily make changes to accommodate all genders or gender identification.

It is preferred (though not absolutely necessary) that the First-Degree Initiation be conferred for three Candidates at a time, certain parts of the ceremony being designed for each individual and parts for them as a group.

IMPORTANT NOTE ON SAFETY:

O∴ H∴ O∴ initiations should never (at any time before, during, or after the ceremony) be the occasion to frighten, belittle, or humiliate the Candidate, who, at all times, shall be treated with the utmost courtesy and respect.

O∴ H∴ O∴
Our Holy Order

CEREMONY OF INITIATION
FIRST-DEGREE
Officer's Script

Figure 1.

OFFICERS

HONORED TEACHER (**HT**): Black hooded robe (hood not worn).

WORTHY GUIDE (**WG**): Black hooded robe (hood not worn).

MUSICIAN (needed for Fifth Section only): Black hooded robe (hood up, covering face).

Candidate is dressed in street clothes throughout this ritual.

Sign, Grip, and Word of the First-Degree

The First-Degree *Sign* is given as follows: right thumb on one's own right eyelid; right middle finger on left eyelid; right forefinger on center of forehead (third eye).

The First-Degree *Grip* is given by linking the first, second, and third fingers of the right hands and squeezing affectionately.

The First-Degree *Word* is "A M Sh" (*Aleph Mem Shin*) and is exchanged in three parts as follows:

- Both initiates give the *Grip*;

- Both initiates make the *Sign* and remain holding the Sign as they exchange the threefold Word;

- The first says, "A" (pronounced "Ah!" with a suggestion of delighted surprise);

- The next responds by saying, "M" (pronounced as an extended "Mmmmmmmm!" intoned with a suggestion of delighted satisfaction);

- Finally, both say together, "Sh" (as an extended "Shhhhhhh!" intoned as a prolonged hush).

Miscellaneous items to have on hand for the ceremony:

- Blindfold
- For each Candidate:
  - Toy: Three pipe cleaners (yellow, blue, red)
  - First-Degree Study Portfolio
  - Pitch pipe
  - Blank journal

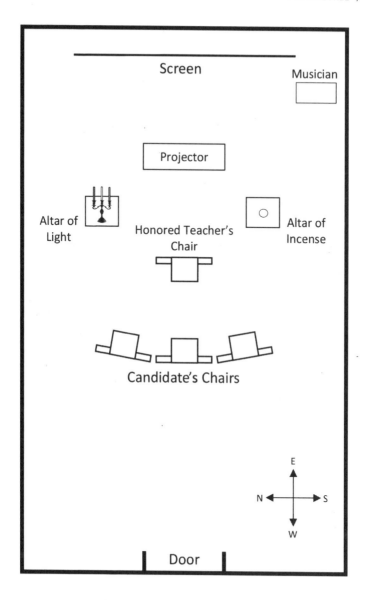

FIGURE 2. FIRST-DEGREE TEMPLE.

IMPORTANT NOTE ON TEMPLE DIRECTIONS:

Temple directions called out in the script—north, south, east, and west—are consistent with the small compass image shown on the Temple floorplan (Figure 2). They are *not to be confused* with the names of the directions associated with the various Hebrew letters that are sometimes referred to in the lectures.

- In the East stands a large projection *screen*. A projector rests on a small table in front of the screen at an appropriate distance to project images on the screen.

- To the South of the screen is concealed the Musician's station. Ideally, the Musician is never seen by the Candidate. The Musician's role is to play particular tonal pitches upon an organ or other such electronic musical instrument. The Musician also remotely operates the projector, changing images projected on the screen at specified cued moments in the ceremony.

- Slightly west of the projector is the *Chair of the Honored Teacher.*

- In the North, on the right hand of the Honored Teacher's chair, is the *Altar of Light*, upon which sits a candelabra holding (for this degree) *three lighted candles*—yellow, blue, and red.

- In the South, on the left hand of the Honored Teacher's chair, is the *Altar of Incense*, upon which rests a censer of smoking frankincense or other sweet-smelling resinous wood gum.

- There are other chairs, one for each Candidate, placed before the Honored Teacher, and positioned so that the Candidates can easily view images on the screen in the East.

- Temple remains dark, illuminated only by the three candles upon the Altar of Light, and by whatever light may be reflected from images projected upon the screen.

- Musical and tonal cues are played during certain sections of the ceremony. An organ (or electronic device) and a remote-control device for the projector are concealed in a place convenient for the Musician to operate.

First-Degree Initiations are ideally performed for three Candidates. They wait comfortably in a *waiting area*[1] outside the Temple proper, until brought in by the Worthy Guide. Candidates are dressed in street clothes and are instructed to remain silent until the Worthy Guide collects them one at a time.

FIRST-DEGREE

I

OPENING CEREMONY

[The screen is BLACK and will remain so during this section.]

[There are no musical cues for this section of the ceremony.]

Candidates are sequestered in the waiting area without the Temple. Because they are not yet First-Degree Initiates, they are not allowed to witness the Opening ceremony.

The Opening ceremony is performed by the Honored Teacher (HT) and Worthy Guide (WG).

> *[WG goes to the Altar of Light and lights the three candles (in order, yellow, blue, red); then goes to the Altar of Incense and ignites the charcoal and frankincense; then moves to stand before HT, who is seated in the Honored Teacher's chair.]*

HT: *[Claps three times.]*
Worthy Guide, what is the hour?

WG:
No hour, Honored Teacher. We dwell in *timelessness* before the birth of Creation.

HT: *[Claps three times.]*
Worthy Guide, what is this place?

WG:
No place, Honored Teacher. We are poised at the *Formless Primal Center of Creation Yet-To-Be.*

HT: *[Claps three times.]*
Worthy Guide, what is the *Formless Primal Center?*

WG:
Honored Teacher, it is hidden from me.

HT:
Worthy Guide, what God shall create limitless space from the dimension-less center? What God shall bring forth *form* from formlessness? What God shall fashion *time* from timelessness?

WG:
The *Number Three*—through the agency of the *Three Mother Letters* of the sacred Hebrew alphabet. *Three* creates Space, Form, and Time, but in doing so shall cast a spell of illusion.

HT:
What are the Three Mother Letters?

WG:
Aleph, Mem, and Shin.

HT:
Where does the letter *Aleph* extend?

WG: *[Places right hand upon the heart and smoothly raises it in a vertical line over the throat, chin, mouth, nose, forehead, and over the head as high as possible while saying . . .]*
From the Center to Infinite Height . . .

WG: *[Cont.] [Places right hand upon the heart and smoothly lowers it in a vertical line over the solar plexus, the navel, and as low as possible while saying . . .]*
. . . and from the Center to Infinite Depth. Ah!

> *[WG intones "Ah" with a suggestion of delighted surprise.]*

HT:
Where does the letter *Mem* extend?

WG: *[Places right hand upon the heart and sweeps the hand and arm horizontally to the right while saying . . .]*
From the Center to the Infinite East . . .[2]

WG: *[Cont.] [Places left hand upon the heart and sweeps the hand and arm horizontally to the left (forming a cross with the body and arms) while saying . . .]*
. . . and from the Center to the Infinite West. Mmmmmmm!

[WG intones "Mmmmmmmmm" with a
suggestion of delighted satisfaction.]

HT:
Where does the letter *Shin* extend?

WG: *[Places both hands upon the heart then pushes them forward saying . . .]*
From the Center to the Infinite North . . .

WG: *[Cont.] [Places both hands upon the heart, then rotates body to a complete "about face," and pushes them forward saying . . .]*
. . . and from the Center to the Infinite South. Shhhhhhhh!

[WG intones "Shhhhhhh" as a prolonged hush.]

[HT stands and faces WG. Both then simultaneously give First-Degree Sign.[3] They then exchange the First-Degree Grip. They hold the Grip as they exchange the First-Degree Word.]

HT:
Ahhhhhh!

WG: *[Answers]*
Mmmmmmmm!

HT & WG: *[Together]*
Shhhhhhhh!

HT:
The Sign is made. The Grip is given. The Word is spoken. I declare the Temple open in the First-Degree.

[HT takes his seat.]

HT: *[Claps three times.]*
The Temple is builded. Worthy Guide, invite the sleeping God to enter and dwell within.

II

RECEPTION OF THE CANDIDATE

[The screen is BLACK and will remain so during this section.]

[There are no musical cues for this section of the ceremony.]

[When more than one Candidate is being initiated, each goes through this section alone; then they return together for Sections IV and V.]

[WG goes without and summons the first Candidate and guides him or her to a place just outside the Temple door.]

WG: *[Speaking in a soft yet solemn tone of voice]*
Is it your will to be received into the Mysteries of Our Holy Order?

CANDIDATE:
Yes.[4]

WG:
Then your Will be done! Take your shoes from off your feet, for the place whereon you stand is holy ground.

[Candidate removes shoes.][5]

WG:
Earthly eyes cannot behold the Light and Beauty of Qabalah!

[WG hands Candidate the blindfold.]

WG: *[Cont.]*
You, and you alone, bear the responsibility for your own condition of blindness. Hold this blindfold firmly over your eyes with the fingertips of both hands.

[WG helps Candidate if necessary.]

[Done.]

WG: *[Cont.]*
Earthly ears cannot hear the pure Music of Qabalah! You, and you alone, bear the responsibility for your own condition of deafness. Cover your ears with the thumbs of both hands.

[WG helps Candidate if necessary.]

[Done.]

[WG opens the door and carefully leads the self-blinded and self-deafened candidate into the darkened Temple. They halt before the Chair of the Honored Teacher. Officers speak loudly so the Candidate may hear.]

WG: *[Claps three times.]*

HT:
Who is this?

WG:
Honored Teacher, standing before you is *"Yah,"*[6] God of all Creation. But she has fallen asleep and has forgotten she is God. In her dreams, she cannot see her own Light or hear the Music of her own Creation.

HT:
Hail unto thee, *"Yah,"* God of all Creation; Divine One—beyond whom Nothing is, and without whom no *thing* can be.

You have fallen into the deepest slumber. What you mistakenly believe to be your life as a mortal woman is a masquerade—a dream life within a dream life within a dream life. Even the words you hear me speaking are dream words. They are but the faintest echoes of a truth—a truth that can be for you good tidings of great joy.

Divine One—you have cursed yourself to remain asleep until you *Will* to awaken. Divine One—you and you alone can arouse yourself from this self-imposed prison of dreams.

O Divine *"Yah,"* God of all Creation, I ask you—is it truly your Will to break your own curse and awaken and remember who you are?

[Officers wait for the Candidate to say "Yes."][7]

CANDIDATE:
Yes.

HT:
Then your Will be done! First, you must *open your own ears* in order to hear the Wisdom of the Holy Teachings.

[WG helps Candidate remove his or her thumbs from over the ears. WG takes care to keep Candidate's fingers holding the blindfold in place over the eyes.]

HT: *[Cont.]*
Listen to the Silence.

[All remain absolutely silent for approximately one minute.]

HT: *[Cont.]*
Instruction is found in the noise of speech. But the Wisdom of the Holy Teachings is heard only in the Silence.

[All remain silent for a moment longer.]

HT: *[Cont.]*
Now uncover your own eyes so that you may behold the Light and Beauty of the Holy Teachings.

[Candidate removes the blindfold, but instead of seeing light sees only the blackness of the screen and the dimly lit HT.]

[HT stands, approaches the Candidate, applies the "Touch of Awakening".]

THE TOUCH OF AWAKENING:

HT gently touches Candidate's right eyelid (with right thumb) and says:
   Ah!

HT touches Candidate's left eyelid (with right middle finger) and says:
   Mmmmmmm!

HT touches center of Candidate's forehead (with right index finger) and says:
   Shhhhhhhh!

[After giving the Touch of Awakening, HT points to the black screen and makes exaggerated gestures of awe, shielding his eyes as if the screen is emanating a blinding light.]

HT:
Behold the Blinding Light of Creation!

[HT turns to the confused Candidate and continues.]

HT: *[Cont.]*
Forms and shapes and colors hide the Soul of Creation. But the Beauty of the Holy Teachings is revealed equally in the Darkness and the Light.

HT: *[Secretly using the Grip of the First-Degree, HT shakes the hand of the Candidate and says:]*
Friend and Comrade, welcome to Our Holy Order.

HT: *[Cont.]*
Please take your seat in our Temple and quietly meditate while we receive your fellows.

[Candidate is allowed to witness the reception of her fellows.]

[Pause.]

[When all have been received . . .]

WG: *[Claps three times.]*
All rise.

HT:
Dear Friends and Comrades, I congratulate you on successfully persevering thus far in the ordeals of your initiation. I observe that you might appreciate a short pause in the formalities so that you may refresh yourself and gather your strength for the challenges that await you. Your Worthy Guide will now escort you from the Temple to a place of rest and refreshment. Upon your return, I will communicate to you the secret keys that unlock the mysteries of this degree, after which we shall proceed with our work.

*[WG escorts Candidates to the waiting area
and bids them to quietly relax for a few minutes
and enjoy water and light refreshments.]*

[WG returns to Temple.]

III

PENETRATION OF THE TEMPLE
OF THE THREE MOTHERS

[The screen is BLACK and will remain so during this section.]

[There are no musical cues for this section of the ceremony.]

*[As before, Candidates will go through
this section one at a time.]*

HT: *[Rises]*
Worthy Guide, if all is in readiness, escort the first Candidate to the Temple
door.

*[WG goes to waiting area, collects first Candidate, and guides
her to the outside of the Temple door, (which is closed).]*

[WG instructs Candidate to knock loudly three times.]

[Done.]

*[HT rises from his chair and goes to the
door. He does not yet open it.]*

HT: *[Speaking loudly from inside the Temple door]*
Who knocks at the door of the *Temple of the Three Mothers*?

WG: *[Loudly answers from outside the Temple door]*
A Dear Friend and Comrade, who has received the *Touch of Awakening* and
has been duly received in Our Holy Order, and now demands entrance to
the *Temple of the Three Mothers* to be attuned and instructed.

HT: *[From inside the Temple door]*
Does she volunteer of her own free will and accord to undergo the ordeal
that will re-attune the instrument of her soul and trigger her reawakening?

*[Even if the Candidate has heard the question,
WG carefully repeats question.]*

WG: *[To Candidate]*
Do you volunteer of your own free will and accord to undergo the ordeal that
will re-attune the instrument of your soul and trigger your reawakening?

*[If Candidate agrees, WG encourages
her to loudly answer "Yes."]*

CANDIDATE: *[From outside the Temple door]*
YES!

> *[Hearing the Candidate's affirmative answer, HT quickly
> and dramatically swings open the door. This action
> should startle the Candidate. HT greets Candidate
> at the threshold with a warm and loving smile.]*

HT:
I greet you at the threshold of the *Temple of the Three Mothers*! However, before you can penetrate the membrane of our sacred Temple, you must prove to us that you have received the *Touch of Awakening*. Worthy Guide, please instruct our Comrade how to properly give the *Sign* of the First-Degree.

WG: *[Addressing the Candidate]*
The *Sign* of the First-Degree is a self-applied form of the touch the Honored Teacher bestowed upon you when you were first brought to light. It is a triangle shining upon your eyes and forehead. It is given thusly:

Using your *right hand*, place the *thumb* on your *right eyelid*; the *middle finger* on your *left eyelid*; and the *right forefinger* on the *center of your forehead* (or third eye).

> *[Candidate repeats action.]*

WG: *[Cont.]*
Turn now and give the *Sign* to the Honored Teacher.

> *[Done.]*

> *[HT returns the Sign.]*

HT:
This *Sign* demands a *Grip*. It is the *Grip* I secretly used when I first welcomed you to Our Holy Order. It is the Key that unlocks the *Temple of the Three Mothers*. It is given by linking the first, second, and third fingers of the right hands and squeezing affectionately.

> *[HT, (still standing inside the threshold of the Temple,) reaches
> his right hand across the threshold and seizes the Candidate's
> right hand with the Grip of the First-Degree. He holds it
> firmly for a moment; then HT vigorously pulls the Candidate
> across the threshold and all the way into the Temple. Ideally,
> this maneuver pulls the Candidate awkwardly off-balance
> and evokes a startled reaction of trepidation and surprise.]*

> *[WG follows Candidate into the Temple and closes door.]*

HT:

This *Grip* demands a *Word*. It is the *Word* which I used to seal the *Touch of Awakening*. Two initiates are required to properly communicate the *Word*. The Worthy Guide and I will demonstrate for you.

> *[HT stands and faces WG. Then both simultaneously give the First-Degree Sign. They then exchange the First-Degree Grip. They hold the Grip as they exchange the First-Degree Word.]*

HT:
Ah!

WG: *[Answers]*
Mmmmmmm!

HT & WG: *[Together]*
Shhhhhhhh!

> *[HT faces Candidate.]*

HT:

The *Word* of the First-Degree is "A M Sh." It is a true magick word composed of the *Three Mother Letters* of the sacred Hebrew alphabet. Before you advance to the Second-Degree, you will have become "Master of the Three Letters." The *Word* is exchanged in three parts. You will now practice with the Worthy Guide, as I describe the procedure.

> *[Candidate again faces WG.]*

HT: *[Cont.]*
After both have made the *Sign* and given the *Grip*, the first says, "A," pronounced "Ah!" and said with a suggestion of delighted surprise.

> *[Candidate says, "Ah!"]*

HT: *[Cont.]*
The second answers by saying "M," pronounced as an extended "Mmmmmmm" and said with a suggestion of delighted satisfaction.

> *[WG says, "Mmmmmmmm."]*

HT: *[Cont.]*
Finally, both say together "Sh," pronounced as a prolonged hush.

> *[Candidate and WG say together, "Shhhhhh"*
> *and then both release the Grip.]*

HT: *[Cont.]*
Dear Friend and Comrade, these are the Signs and Tokens whereby one initiate of Our Holy Order may know another. While these actions

appear on the surface to be childish and whimsical, I assure you, the magical significance of these simple gestures and words is profound and powerful. Memorize them. Meditate upon them. You are required to prove proficient in their execution in order to gain admission to a First-Degree Temple.

More importantly, you will most assuredly be called upon to employ them as magick gestures that serve to open doors and unlock mysterious levels of consciousness in your own dreams and astral visions. They are the secret Signs and Words that unlock doors between levels of consciousness.

I now invite you to take your seat in the Temple.

[Done.]

[Candidate takes her seat and witnesses the others (if any come this far). They all then remain seated for the Welcoming Lecture.]

IV

WELCOMING LECTURE

HT:
Dear Friends and Comrades, I compliment you on your steadfast willingness to undergo the confusion and discomforts which you have cheerfully endured so far. I assure you it is not our objective to embarrass you with childish ordeals or torment you with make-believe horrors. Rather, it is our intention to offer you experiences designed to fundamentally and profoundly modify your psyche, so you may grow more perfectly attuned to the fundamental harmonies of creation.

Our Holy Order has no name. We do not claim to be an ancient and formal mystery school with thousands of members around the world. Rather, we meet and work only when and where our dreams intersect.

In truth, *you* are the only member of Our Holy Order. *You* are the Honored Teacher. *You* are the Worthy Guide. *You* are the Temple, and *you* are the Teachings. You are the Shrine, and you are the God within the Shrine.

For the moment, however, you are not yet awake enough to realize that the words I speak are true. So, for the time being, simply continue to embrace your role in a dream in which you are the newest initiated member of "Our Holy Order," a modern Mystery School created just for *you*.

I caution you, however: Do not misjudge the underlying motives of our pleasant and casual approach to the subject of Qabalah. Do not think that just because we laugh and take playful delight in our labor that we are not a real initiatory society engaged in serious work on a cosmic scale. Painless and undemanding as your experience today has been, you are, even now, undergoing true and profound initiation. This is not something *we* are doing to you. Rather, it is something you are doing to yourself. You have willfully placed your foot upon the path, and by doing so, you have triggered an unstoppable chain of events. Nothing in heaven or earth can now prevent you from arriving inevitably at your destination.

In the past, mystery schools and initiatory orders operated as secret societies whose members were bound by terrible oaths to be obedient to the superiors of the order, and sworn to secrecy as to the nature of the work. Perhaps in the past there were good reasons for such obedience and secrecy, but Our Holy Order will never demand any such promises from you. At each step of your initiatory career, your only oath shall be to *yourself* and to yourself alone—a pledge to awaken—a pledge to become truly self-aware.

Qabalah teaches that each one of us is the perfect "image" of God. When we come to full realization of who we are—when we wake up—we will realize that we are not merely the image of God, we are in essence . . . *God*. That is why, in the ceremony you just experienced, you were introduced as "*Yah*," one of many names for the Supreme Singularity of Being. From your studies, you will recall that "Yah" is the special Name of God, spoken of in the opening verse of the *Sepher Yezirah*; the God that initiates the opening sequences of Creation by means of ten numbers and twenty-two letters.

But at the moment, as we will repeatedly remind you, you are not awake to your true divine nature. You are asleep and dreaming you are in a dream . . . inside a dream . . . inside many other dreams.

I cannot wake you up. *Worthy Guide* cannot wake you up. *Qabalah* cannot wake you up. *Death* cannot wake you up. *Reincarnation* cannot wake you up. Only when you open your heart and mind; only when you begin the process of tuning up the sleep-rusted moving parts of your soul; only when you lubricate your consciousness with the anointing oil of orderly madness that is *Qabalah* will you begin again . . . *to think like God*.

No matter how much we try to *teach* you, we cannot *teach* you how to think like God.

No matter how long and hard you *study*, you cannot *study* how to think like God.

You can only *remember* how to think like God.

My Qabalah is not, and will never be, *your* Qabalah—and you will proceed in your work in your own unique way. Each of us slumber and dream our own particular dream; so, each of us must awaken in our own particular way.

If you are seriously attracted to Qabalah, you will, in the coming months and years, collect and read scores of books about Qabalah. We will, of course, recommend those texts which will initially be most helpful to your ongoing self-education. But all these reference works will be meaningless to you, unless you have first started the process of remembering how to think like God. *That* is the purpose of Our Holy Order, and that is all we promise to offer you.

I now ask you: Do you accept this promise and wish to continue?

[HT waits for Candidates to answer "Yes."]

CANDIDATES:
Yes.

HT: *[Cont.]*
At each step of the process, it is you who must make the first move. Are you ready to begin? Are you ready to take the great Oath to yourself right now?

[HT waits for Candidates to answer "Yes."]

CANDIDATES:
Yes.

HT: *[Cont.]*
Very well. Please stand up and give the First-Degree Sign . . .

[Candidates stand and give First-Degree Sign.]

HT: *[Cont.]*
. . . and say after me: "I solemnly and sincerely promise myself that I will awaken to the true essence of my being."

[Candidates repeat Oath.]

HT: *[Cont.]*
Thank you. Please be seated.

I will be frank with you. At the beginning of your journey, our teachings and assignments will seem strange, confusing, and probably, for many of you . . . dreadfully *boring*. You will not immediately understand *why* you are learning and memorizing so many seemingly useless things. You will probably ask yourself, "Do all Qabalists feel so bewildered and confused at the beginning?" The simple answer is,

> *"Hell yes!*
>
> *Don't worry about it!"*[8]

The Hebrew Qabalah has a thousand-year traditional history among scholars and intellectuals of the Jewish religion. Like the illuminated masters of every age and culture, the ancient Qabalists were aware that God and the secrets of God are present in all things at all times. Nevertheless, for various reasons, certain passionately religious Qabalists chose to focus their investigations exclusively on the books of their own culture's sacred scriptures to extract infinite wisdom and divine mysteries from every letter and word written therein. They associated the letters of their language to numbers so that they might glean more wisdom from the elegant beauty and music of mathematics.

The ancient Jewish Qabalists elevated their art and practice to breathtaking heights of intellectual complexity, but in their religious zeal, some of them became blind to the universality of the Great Work. They became "stiff-necked" and dogmatic, asserting the wisdom of Qabalah can be found only in *their own* scriptures. They lost sight of the fundamental truth outlined in our *Tenth Command-Rant:*[9] "Look hard enough at *anything* and you will eventually see *everything.*"

In their hubris, they fell to worshipping the tools of Qabalah, rather than the universal God within themselves that those tools were designed to reveal. I regret to say that, even today, there are those who insist that in order to study Qabalah, you must be an observant Jew. There are those who will dogmatically insist that women are forbidden to study Qabalah. There are those who sincerely believe that only a *married man* over forty years of age (who has fathered at least one male child) . . . who must own his own home, and have servants so that he does not have to wash clothes or cook food or clean can study Qabalah.

Dear Friends and Comrades, I ask you: How many of us can say we are able to fulfill these requirements? I certainly cannot.

We should always honor and respect the rights of others to their sincere and heartfelt beliefs. But there is a dramatic difference between pious "Bible Scholars" and impartial academic scholars; and there is a profound difference between "Traditional Biblical history" and "empirical and objectively verifiable history." Modern scholars are almost universal in their assertion that the fundamentals of Qabalistic thought are not the exclusive heritage of any one particular religion or culture. Indeed, the fundamentals can be traced far back in time . . . even to the Sumerians. In fact, what is commonly known as the Jewish Qabalah actually first developed from the mystic *Greek* philosophers and their ingenious marriage of the Greek alphabet to sacred numbers.

Like the Greeks, Jewish mystics used their alphabets to link letters and words to numbers and explored the qualities and relationships of numbers in order to connect every idea and concept in the universe with every other idea and concept in the universe.

In the twelfth and thirteenth centuries, Muslim and Christian mystics were exposed to the Greek and Hebrew Qabalahs, and soon began to understand how this marvelous way of organizing human thought could be applied to their spiritual traditions. In the late 1800s, German and English magicians, especially the magicians of the *Hermetic Order of the Golden Dawn*, gathered up universal concepts shared by many of the world's mythologies and religions; they organized and classified their mysteries on a scaffolding of the Hebrew alphabet and the numbers represented by the letters. It is this material that primarily forms the basis of modern Qabalistic practice. And it is this material that we will be working with in Our Holy Order.

Qabalah is not a religion. It matters not what religion you are, or even if you embrace no religion at all. You don't have to believe in the objective reality of gods or angels or demons or spirits. Ultimately, concepts such as gods, angels, demons, spirits, scriptures, words, letters, and numbers are merely colorful metaphors that can bring to life in your imagination the infinite and formless facets of the Supreme Consciousness.

As modern Qabalists, we honor and embrace the living allegories of our ancient and orthodox predecessors. Used skillfully, the traditional god-names and archangels and angels and spirits and demons serve, as they have always served, as elegant and dramatic tools of consciousness expansion. We must *not*, however, allow ourselves to again fall victim to the ancient curse of superstitiously objectifying these sacred abstractions and creating for ourselves yet another silly *belief system*—and imprisoning ourselves in deeper and deeper layers of dream.

The most *we* will ever ask of you is that you simply believe in yourself.

Dear Friends and Comrades, do you believe in yourself?

*[**All** answer, "Yes."]*

HT:

I now observe that you are growing restless and would like to take time to digest your experience so far. We will now pause in our labors so that we may rest and refresh ourselves with a delightful evening meal[10] and entertainment. The Worthy Guide and I invite you to be our guest in the banquet hall. Afterward, we ask that you return to your room and relax, bathe, and perhaps even take a refreshing nap. We will meet again outside the Temple door shortly before midnight and proceed with the final section of your First-Degree Initiation.

HT: *[Claps three times.]*

WG:

All rise. Please follow me.

[WT extinguishes the three candles, but the Temple remains technically "open" during this lengthy break.]

V

CEREMONY OF THE LOST CHORD

[The screen is BLACK at the beginning of this section, but as HT proceeds with the guided meditation, the MUSICIAN will cycle through projected colors and images indicated by slide number.]

[Simultaneous to the visual changes on the screen, the MUSICIAN will also play specific notes on the organ or electronic device.][11]

SLIDE # ?[12]

Total blackness.

[Prior to the Candidate's return, WG unceremoniously relights the three candles on the Altar of Light and ignites fresh charcoal and frankincense upon the Altar of Incense. The room should be heavy with incense smoke.]

[After the Candidates have eaten dinner, relaxed, and bathed, they gather outside the Temple door shortly before

*midnight. They are met by the WG, who thoroughly
"tests" each Candidate for the proper Sign, Grip, and
Word of the Degree, after which they are invited to
take their seats in the Temple facing the screen.]*

HT:
Welcome back to the final section of your First-Degree Initiation. We hope
you are well restored and refreshed by your meal and bath, and are now
ready to undergo a wondrous and magical meditation.

I want you to relax and for a few minutes simply enjoy your own imagination and powers of visualization. Take a few deep breaths and focus
your attention on the black emptiness you see upon the screen. Clear your
mind and become as serene and empty as the peaceful darkness you see
on the screen. When you are able to capture and project this black emptiness on the screen of your mind's eye, *close your eyes . . .* and watch . . .
and listen.

....

MUSIC

*Starting at a very low and soothing volume level,
MUSICIAN plays the deepest, lowest A note[13] possible.
Ideally, this A note should be of such a low frequency
that it is nearly inaudible . . . a background hum.
This note is sustained until the next music cue.*

....

HT:
Worthy Guide, what is the hour?

WG:
No hour, Honored Teacher. We dwell in *timelessness* before the birth of
Creation.

HT:
Worthy Guide, what is this place?

WG:
No place, Honored Teacher. We are poised at the *Formless Primal Center of
Creation Yet-To-Be.*

HT:
Please *open your eyes* and behold the Formless Primal Center of Creation
Yet-To-Be. When you can capture and project this image on the screen of
your mind's eye, *close your eyes* once again.

....
SLIDE # ?

A small white ring in the center of the black screen.
....
MUSIC

*MUSICIAN continues to hold the sustained low A but
now adds a mid-range A to form a simple chord.*
....

HT:
Worthy Guide, what *is* the Formless Primal Center?

WG:
Honored Teacher, it is hidden.

HT:
Yes, it is hidden. It is the hidden center of *nonexistent Nothingness.* No
inside. No outside. No *"it."* No *"is."* This dimensionless point . . . this posi-
tionless singularity . . . this Formless Primal Center . . . is YOU . . . the
REAL YOU, and from *you* all will proceed; and unto you all shall return.

[Pause.]

As you visualize this simple image in your mind's eye, I want you to project
your full consciousness and everything you *think you are* into the center of
this point. Identify completely with this point. It is YOU—and there is no
inside of you; there is no outside of you. Just . . . *you.*
....
SLIDE # ?

Screen turns bright pale yellow.
....
MUSIC

Changes to mid-range E.[14]
....

[Pause.]

HT:
When you have firmly identified yourself as this point, *open your eyes* and
behold the color of dawning self-awareness. When you are able to capture
and project this pure color yellow on the screen of your mind's eye, *close
your eyes* once again.

[Pause.]

HT: *[Cont.]*
Worthy Guide, what is happening?

WG:
The Beginning.

HT:
The Beginning of what?

WG:
The Beginning of Existence itself. The Beginning of *Being*; the Beginning of *Space* . . . and *Form* . . . and *Time*.

HT:
Let us visualize this pure yellow focusing into the heart of the Formless Primal Center . . . then bursting and *rising* straight up as a *scintillating* and *fiery* yellow ray of light. As it rises higher and higher from your center, it creates the infinitely extending dimension of the *Above*.

....

MUSIC

Highest E possible.

....

WG:
Honored Teacher, how high up does the yellow ray of the Above ascend?

HT:
Worthy Guide, it ascends forever. It ascends to *Infinite Height* and seals the direction by virtue of its eternal extension.

[Pause.]

HT: *[Cont.]*
Keeping your *eyes closed*, visualize the pure yellow bursting again from the Formless Primal Center—but now *descending* as a yellow ray of light. As it plunges lower and lower from the center, it creates the infinitely extending dimension of the *Below*.

....

MUSIC

Lowest E possible.

....

WG:
Honored Teacher, how low down does the yellow ray descend?

HT:
Worthy Guide, it descends forever. It descends to *Infinite Depth* and seals the direction by virtue of its eternal extension.

[Pause.]

HT: *[Cont.]*

Now, continue to visualize this vertical yellow ray of light extending simultaneously upward and downward from your Formless Primal Center. Feel your head stretching higher and higher while your feet and legs stretch lower and lower.

[Pause.]

HT: *[Cont.]*

Worthy Guide, does the infinitely extending yellow line of height and depth have a name?

WG:

It has, Worthy Teacher. Its name is "Aleph," and it is the first of the *Three Mother Letters* of the Hebrew alphabet. Aleph is the letter that creates and weds Above and Below.

HT:

Open your eyes and behold Aleph. Feel yourself as Aleph.

א [Heb: Aleph]

....

MUSIC

Mid-range E held.

....

SLIDE # ?

*Large, bright, pale yellow Aleph against
a pale mauve background.*

....

HT:

The extension of Aleph creates Above and Below.

[Pause.]

WG:

Gaze deeply at the Sacred Letter *Aleph*. Don't take your eyes from it.

[Pause.]

....

SLIDE # ?

*Slide changes to bright white; in doing so, creates a floating
pale mauve ghost image of Aleph in the Candidate's brain.*[15]

....

[Pause.]

HT:
See now, with the eyes of your soul, the true color and image of Aleph. Close your eyes and implant Aleph deep in the center of your brain.[16]

[Pause.]

[HT gets up and presents a yellow pipe cleaner to each seated Candidate.]

HT: *[Cont.]*
Aleph—Hold it vertically between your thumb and forefinger at the center of the ray.

Aleph—The letter that creates and weds Above and Below.

Now I want you to again close your eyes and project your full consciousness and everything you *think you are* into the center point.

....

SLIDE # ?

Screen turns deep blue.

....

MUSIC

Changes to mid-range G♯.

....

[Pause.]

HT:
When you have firmly identified yourself as this point, open your eyes and behold the next color of dawning self-awareness. When you are able to capture and project this pure deep blue on the screen of your mind's eye, close your eyes once again.

[Pause.]

HT: *[Cont.]*
Worthy Guide, what is happening?

WG:
The second phase of the Beginning.

HT:
The Beginning of what?

WG:
The Beginning of Existence itself. The Beginning of Being; the Beginning of *Space* . . . and *Form* . . . and *Time.*

HT:

Let us visualize this deep blue focusing into the heart of the Formless Primal Center, then bursting and shooting *to your right* as a *firm* and *stable* ray of blue light. As it extends from your center, it creates the infinitely extending dimension of the *East*.

WG:

Honored Teacher, how far does the blue ray of *the East* extend?

HT:

Worthy Guide, it extends forever. It extends infinitely Eastward and seals the direction by virtue of its eternal extension.

[Pause.]

HT: *[Cont.]*

Now let us visualize the deep blue ray bursting again from your Formless Primal Center—but now shooting to your *left* as a *firm* and *stable* ray of blue light. As it extends from your center, it creates the infinitely extending dimension of the West.

WG:

Honored Teacher, how far to *the West* does the blue ray extend?

HT:

Worthy Guide, it extends forever. It extends infinitely Westward and seals the direction by virtue of its eternal extension.

[Pause.]

HT: *[Cont.]*

Now let us continue to visualize this horizontal blue ray of light extending simultaneously right and left from your Formless Primal Center. Feel your hands and arms stretching on and on toward infinite East and West.

[Pause.]

HT: *[Cont.]*

Worthy Guide, does the infinitely extending blue line of East and West have a name?

[Pause.]

WG:

It has, Worthy Teacher. Its name is "Mem," and it is the second of the *Three Mother Letters* of the Hebrew alphabet. Mem is the letter that creates and weds East and West.

HT:
Open your eyes and behold Mem. Feel yourself as Mem.

מ [Heb: Mem]

....

MUSIC

Mid-range G# held.

....

SLIDE # ?

Large, deep blue Mem against a bright orange background.

....

HT:
The extension of Mem creates East and West.

[Pause.]

WG:
Gaze deeply at the Sacred Letter *Mem.* Don't take your eyes from it.

[Pause.]

....

SLIDE # ?

Slide changes to bright white; in doing so, creates a floating orange ghost image of Mem in the Candidate's brain.

....

[Pause.]

HT:
See now, with the eyes of your soul, the true color and image of Mem. *Close your eyes* and implant Mem deep in the center of your brain.

[Pause.]

[HT gets up and presents a blue pipe cleaner to each seated Candidate.]

HT:
Mem—Hold it horizontally between your thumb and forefinger at the center of the ray, making a perfect cross with the yellow ray of Aleph.

Now I want you to again close your eyes and project your full consciousness and everything you *think you are* into the center point.

....

SLIDE # ?

Screen turns scarlet red.

....

MUSIC

Changes to mid-range C.[17]

....

[Pause.]

HT:
When you have firmly identified yourself as this point, *open your eyes* and behold the next color of dawning self-awareness. When you are able to capture and project this scarlet red on the screen of your mind's eye, *close your eyes* once again.

[Pause.]

HT: *[Cont.]*
Worthy Guide, what is happening?

WG:
The Final phase of the Beginning.

HT:
The Beginning of what?

WG:
The Beginning of Existence itself. The Beginning of Being; the Beginning of *Space* . . . and *Form* . . . and *Time*.

HT:
Let us visualize this pure red focusing into the heart of the Formless Primal Center, then bursting and shooting *directly in front of you* as a *Perpetually Radiant* ray of scarlet red light. As it extends from your center, it creates the infinitely extending dimension of the *North*.

WG:
Honored Teacher, how far does the scarlet red ray of *the North* extend?

HT:
Worthy Guide, it extends forever. It extends infinitely Northward and seals the direction by virtue of its eternal extension.

[Pause.]

HT: *[Cont.]*
Now let us visualize the scarlet red ray bursting again from your Formless Primal Center—but now shooting directly *behind you* as a *Perpetually Radiant* ray of red light. As it extends from your center, it creates the infinitely extending dimension of the South.

WG:
Honored Teacher, how far to *the South* does the scarlet red ray extend?

HT:
Worthy Guide, it extends forever. It extends infinitely Southward and seals the direction by virtue of its eternal extension.

[Pause.]

HT: *[Cont.]*
Now let us continue to visualize this horizontal scarlet red ray of light extending simultaneously North and South from your Formless Primal Center. Feel your chest and your spine stretching on and on toward infinite North and South.

[Pause.]

HT: *[Cont.]*
Worthy Guide, does the infinitely extending red line of North and South have a name?

[Pause.]

WG:
It has, Worthy Teacher. Its name is "Shin," and it is the third of the *Three Mother Letters* of the Hebrew alphabet. Shin is the letter that creates and weds North and South.

HT:
Open your eyes and behold Shin. Feel yourself as Shin.

שׁ [Heb: Shin]

....
MUSIC

Mid-range C held.
....
SLIDE # ?

Large, red Shin against a bright green background.
....

HT: *[Cont.]*
The extension of Shin creates North and South.

[Pause.]

WG:
Gaze deeply at the Sacred Letter *Shin.* Don't take your eyes from it.

[Pause.]

....

SLIDE # ?

*Slide changes to bright white; in doing so, creates a floating
green ghost image of Shin in the Candidate's brain.*

....

[Pause.]

HT:

See now, with the eyes of your soul, the true color and image of Shin. *Close
your eyes* and implant Shin deep in the center of your brain.

[Pause.]

*[HT gets up and presents a red pipe cleaner
to each seated Candidate.]*

HT:

Shin—Hold it diagonally and obliquely between your thumb and forefinger
at the center of the yellow and blue cross of Aleph and Mem.

Shin—The letter that creates and weds North and South.

....

SLIDE # ?

*Hebrew letters: yellow Aleph, blue Mem, and
red Shin above the threefold cross.*

....

אמש

FIGURE 3.

HT:
Take a moment now to twist your three pipe cleaners together. First join the yellow and blue (for Aleph and Mem), forming the dimensional cross of Above/Below and East/West; then join the red pipe cleaner of Shin at the center of the cross to form the dimension of North/South.

> *[HT and WG assist Candidates to properly*
> *form their three pipe cleaners to form a "star"*
> *of Up–Down / East–West / North–South.]*

HT: *[Cont.]*
Let this simple toy remind you that the Three Mother Letters create creation itself. Without *Three*, the Beginning would not begin. Without *Three*, Space and Time could not unfold.

When you understand the true meaning of this little toy, your soul will be inseminated by the primary pattern of the Supreme Consciousness of Godhead;

When you understand the true meaning of this little toy, the DNA of your soul will be mutated as it begins to vibrate in harmony with the DNA of existence itself;

When you understand the true meaning of this little toy, you will be *Master of the Three Mothers.*

> *[HT is seated.]*

Dear Friends and Comrades, each step toward godhead is an awakening to a completely new reality; a completely new universe; a completely new form of consciousness. You can spend your entire incarnation reading about these steps; you can spend your entire incarnation studying what others have written about these steps; you can spend your entire incarnation memorizing ancient charts and graphs and tables of correspondences that dissect and analyze these steps; you can spend your entire life debating, arguing, preaching, and postulating about the nature of each step of awakening—but unless you actually *awaken,* you labor eternally within a dream; a dream in which the *Tree of Life* remains a map of a fantasy journey you will never begin; a dream in which Qabalah is a never-ending study course in a school from which you can never graduate.

My Friends, all the traditional Qabalistic literature that has been written over the centuries can be fascinating and engaging to our minds. But you will never think like God by reading Qabalistic literature.

All the Qabalistic games we play with numbers and letters are valuable exercises that help us understand and be part of the mechanics of creative consciousness. But you will never think like God by playing games with numbers and letters.

It is the great paradox of Qabalah that study and practice become truly valuable only when you are *already thinking like God.*

Wake up first! Then study!

VI

CLOSING CEREMONY

[The screen is BLACK and will remain so during this section.]

[There are no musical cues for this section of the ceremony.]

[Newly initiated Candidates take part in the Closing ceremony.][18]

HT: *[Claps three times.]*

[All rise.]

Worthy Guide, what is the hour?

WG:
No hour, Honored Teacher. We dwell in *timelessness* before the birth of Creation.

HT: *[Claps three times.]*
Worthy Guide, what is this place?

WG:
No place, Honored Teacher. We are poised at the *Formless Primal Center of Creation Yet-To-Be.*

HT: *[Claps three times.]*
Worthy Guide, what is the *Formless Primal Center?*

WG:
Honored Teacher, it is hidden from me.

HT:
Worthy Guide, what God shall create limitless space from the dimension-less center? What God shall bring forth *form* from formlessness? What God shall fashion *time* from timelessness?

WG:
The *Number Three*—through the agency of the *Three Mother Letters* of the sacred Hebrew alphabet. *Three* creates Space, Form, and Time, but in doing so shall cast a spell of illusion.

HT:
What are the Three Mother Letters?

WG:
Aleph, Mem, and Shin.

HT:
Where does the letter *Aleph* extend?

WG: *[Places right hand upon the heart and smoothly raises it in a vertical line over the throat, chin, mouth, nose, forehead, and over the head as high as possible while saying . . .]*
From the Center to Infinite Height . . .

WG: *[Places right hand upon the heart and smoothly lowers it in a vertical line over the solar plexus, the navel, and as low as possible while saying . . .]*
. . . and from the Center to Infinite Depth. Ah!

> *[WG intones "Ah" with a suggestion of delighted surprise.]*

HT:
Where does the letter *Mem* extend?

WG: *[Places right hand upon the heart and sweeps the hand and arm horizontally to the right while saying . . .]*
From the Center to the Infinite East . . .

WG: *[Places left hand upon the heart and sweeps the hand and arm horizontally to the left while saying . . .]*
. . . and from the Center to the Infinite West. Mmmmmmm!

> *[WG intones "Mmmmmmmm" with a
> suggestion of delighted satisfaction.]*

HT:
Where does the letter *Shin* extend?

WG: *[Places both hands upon the heart, then pushes them forward saying . . .]*
From the Center to the Infinite North . . .

WG: *[Places both hands upon the heart, then rotates body to a complete "about face" and pushes them forward saying . . .]*
. . . and from the Center to the Infinite South. Shhhhhhhh!

[WG intones "Shhhhhhh" as a prolonged hush.]

[All join WG in repeating, "Shhhhhhh!"]

[HT stands and faces WG. Then both simultaneously give the First-Degree Sign. Then they exchange the First-Degree Grip. Then they hold this gesture as they exchange the First-Degree Word.]

HT:
Ahhhhhh!

WG: *[Answers]*
Mmmmmmm!

HT & WG: *[Together]*
Shhhhhhhh!

HT:
The Sign is made. The Grip is given. The Word is Spoken. I declare the Temple closed in the First-Degree. Worthy Guide, extinguish the tapers and withdraw the threefold light back into the *Formless Primal Center of Creation Yet-To-Be.*

[WG extinguishes the three candles (in reverse order—red, blue, yellow).]

HT: *[Claps three times.]*
The Ceremony is ended.

[WG turns on the overhead lights.]

VII

PRESENTATION OF JOURNAL, TOY, AND FIRST-DEGREE PORTFOLIO

HT:
Finally, it gives me great pleasure to present you gifts.

[HT presents each new initiate with a new blank book journal.]

HT: *[Cont.]*
This book is the most important Qabalah book you will ever possess. It is your life's story—your autobiography—your examined life—your confession—your prayer book. It is entirely private. Unless you want to share its contents, this book is for your eyes only.

In it, you will record your daily practices, results, dreams, thoughts, and experiences. Keeping this daily record is important not only to you, but to those who come after you. In a very real sense, this book represents the difference between immortality or a life lived as a windblown puff of smoke.

[HT presents each new initiate with the First-Degree Portfolio.]

HT: *[Cont.]*
This is your First-Degree Study Portfolio. It includes a recommended reading list, charts and graphs, exercises and meditations appropriate to this degree.

It also includes a *pitch pipe,* for you will need it in the coming months.

Most importantly, it contains a complete copy of the *Initiation Ceremony* you have just experienced. Study it well. Of all the materials appointed for your study, it is the most important because, whether you realize it or not, this initiation has mutated you in a most fundamental and wonderful way. Memorize it like a song. Rehearse it daily in your memory and imagination. Relive the details in your mind each night as you compose yourself for sleep. By doing so, you will rouse the soul's dreaming chrysalis to awaken as the divine butterfly of Self.

The Three Mothers Letters are now a fertilized seed that has been imbedded deep in your sleeping soul. It will soon sprout and grow. To assure its vitality, you need only to nurture it with your persistent, loving attention. Do this, and you will surely awaken. When you are Master of the Three Mothers, you will return to us and take the next step to your awakening.

O∴ H∴ O∴
FIRST-DEGREE
Portfolio

Figure 4. First-Degree Candelabra.

FIRST-DEGREE
Study Program

Nothing is too silly or frivolous if it provides the opportunity for you to familiarize yourself with the letters you are assigned to master.

Congratulations upon receiving your First-Degree Initiation. We hope that the ceremony was for you both memorable and edifying and that you feel generally enriched by the experience. The following material is intended to be suggestive of a course of study and practice designed to help you digest and process the mysteries and lessons of the First-Degree and prepare you for the challenges that await you in the next degree.

Hebrew Letter & English	Name #	Full Spelling #	Meaning	Element & Tarot Trump	Color	Flashing Color	Music Note	Qabalistic Intelligence	Direction
א A	Aleph 1	אלף ALP 111	Ox	Air & Fool	Bright Pale Yellow	Pale Mauve	E	Scintillating Intelligence	Up-Down
מ M	Mem 40 or 600 Final ם	מים MIM 90	Sea	Water & Hanged Man	Deep Blue	Bright Orange	G#	Stable Intelligence	East-West Right-Left
ש Sh	Shin 300	שן ShN 350	Teeth	Fire (& element Spirit) & Judgment	Glowing Orange Scarlet	Emerald Green	C	Perpetual Intelligence	North-South Forward-Backward

TABLE 1. TABLE OF THE THREE MOTHER LETTERS.

Perpetual Tinkering

Using the Table of the Three Mother Letters and the reference works in your own Qabalah library,[1] *tinker* with the three letters and their associated numbers in every way imaginable to you. Practice writing them out. Master them with good penmanship. Make them subjects of your mindless doodling as you talk on the phone or wait for a bus.

Add them; subtract them; multiply and divide them. Expand them by their full spellings and explore and trifle with their component letters and numbers. Compound them with other letters (even those whose mysteries have not yet been introduced to you). For these "tinkerings," you will need to refer to other books in your own Qabalah reference library, without which the most fundamental traditional Qabalistic calculations are impossible. For the First-Degree, we especially recommend

- *Sepher Yezirah:*[2] Chapters I, II, and III

- *Chicken Qabalah:* Chapter III

And for other topics of general research:

- The alchemical elements: Mercury, Salt, Sulfur

- The Hindu Gunas: Sattvas, Tamas, Rajas

- The Tarot Card, *Wheel of Fortune;* figures on the rim of the wheel, Hermanubis, Typhon, and Sphinx

- Ideas of the qualities of *Thought, Feeling,* and *Ecstasy*

In your journal, record your discoveries, revelations, or other Qabalistic synchronicities you observe. But, please: don't try to share or explain any of your great revelations to anyone else. Trust me. They won't understand, and you'll be a happier person if you don't even try.

Initiation Script[3]

> *It is your Great Work, as a First-Degree Initiate, to deeply embed this ceremony in your psyche before proceeding to the next degree.*

You are probably still a bit bewildered by all that occurred during your Initiation Ceremony, and that is to be expected. I am well aware that during the ritual it was impossible for you (as a nervous and distracted Candidate) to absorb or properly appreciate all that was at the time said and done to you. Nevertheless, because it is so important that you fully comprehend the importance of your First-Degree experience, I am providing you with a full copy of the *Initiation Script*,[4] which I expect you to study and repeatedly rehearse as part of your daily practices and meditations. If you wish, you may even enlist the help of a friend or two and stage the initiation in your home. It's not secret. Have fun.

Each time you read through the script, you will in essence be reliving your initiation. As you become increasingly familiar with the rhythm and poetry of the ceremony, things that occurred on a *symbolic* level during the Temple ceremony will become *actualized* for you on a spiritual level.

Please pay special attention to the *Opening ceremony* that took place in the Temple before you were brought in. It was how the officers magically prepared the Temple and created a specific environment that resonated in harmony with the formulae of the Three Mother Letters. You are encouraged to customize for yourself a version of the Opening and Closing ceremonies to begin and close your own daily practices and meditations associated with this degree. An example of such an abbreviated ceremony is provided in these notes.

It is also very important that you thoroughly memorize the various Signs, Grips, and Words of the degree until they become as familiar as your favorite song. (Pretend you may someday bump into a fellow initiate in an elevator and would like to prove to each other that you've both passed through the ceremony.)

These tokens are symbolic gestures and words that literally *come alive* and become powerful tools on more subtle planes. Properly mastered and internalized, they can be employed to help you pass from one level of consciousness to another. It is desirable that you become adept in intoning these words and performing these actions even in your dreams and visions. (The ancient Egyptians would go so far as to maintain that you must be able to do them *even when you are dead!*)

First-Degree Toy and Your New Life as an Artist

Your First-Degree toy is the simple object you fashioned from the three *pipe cleaners* you were presented with at the conclusion of your initiation. You will *play* with this toy as a meditation aid when attuning yourself to the Three Mother Letters. You may also wish to create your own, more substantial piece of *art*, a sculpture or a painting of the three-colored "star." Art projects like this are very important for the initiate, who must now also become a *Qabalah artist*.

As I have repeatedly stressed, it is not enough that you be a "Qabalah student" who reads and studies traditional and contemporary literature.

You also must be a "Qabalah artist." Art touches and moves and transforms us at the most primal spiritual levels (which is precisely where we want to be touched and moved and transformed if we want to wake up!). Where Qabalah is concerned, our canvas is consciousness, and our palette is made from the numbers, names, shapes, colors, smells, musical notes, and the associated concepts of everything in the entire universe, as they are organized and categorized by the Hebrew alphabet.

Like it or not, as a First-Degree Initiate, you are now a Qabalah artist. It doesn't matter if you've never picked up a paint brush or a colored pen before in your life. We want you to start doing something like that now! Involving yourself in small, focused, Qabalistic art projects is a serious continuation of your initiatory experience. It is the fastest method—the shortest short-cut, the *laziest lazy person's* way—to firmly embed the magic essence of each letter of the Hebrew alphabet and Qabalistic principles in your soul!

You are totally free (as all artists must be) to design and create your First-Degree, Mother Letter art pieces. Your only restrictions are the various colors, shapes, musical notes, and concepts (objective and abstract) associated with each of the Three Mother Letters.

You can create as many of these projects as you wish, but (because they are going to be necessary tools for one of your First-Degree exercises) there are three very simple art objects you will be required to create.

FIRST-DEGREE ART ASSIGNMENT

Flash Card Color Images of the Three Mother Letters

You will recall that during your initiation you were asked to gaze upon a projected color image of each of the Mother Letters. The image was suddenly withdrawn, leaving a blank white screen upon which floated a "ghost" image of the letter appearing like an apparition of the opposite or "flashing" color.

Colors, as we see them with our physical eyes (and which we interpret by our conscious minds), actually appear to us as such because they absorb all colors *except* the one we are looking at. In other words, what our conscious mind (here on the *material* plane) sees as *red* is really *green* on the *immaterial* plane of consciousness.

Your art assignment for the First-Degree is to create three brightly colored "flash cards," one for each Mother Letter. Do this first by hand, not computer. You will find the names of the appropriate colors itemized on the Table of the Three Mother Letters. For example, for Aleph:

1. On a plain, *bright white* piece of 8½ × 11-inch heavy paper or card stock, lightly trace (in pencil) the outline of a large letter Aleph.

2. Using bright *pale yellow* oil, acrylic, or watercolor paint or pens, carefully fill in the Aleph. Be careful to cover over or otherwise erase the pencil line.

Make two more flash cards—one for Mem (deep blue) and one for Shin (glowing orange scarlet). Also, have a fourth plain, white sheet that will be used in the exercise.

Something to remember as you work on your art projects: Just as a lover will forever subliminally associate a certain fragrance or a certain piece of music with a complex and overwhelmingly powerful romantic memory, so, too, is it desirable that you link as many sensory associations as possible with each of the Hebrew letters.

Even a simple art project takes many hours to create; so, while you are struggling with drafts and other mundane, time-consuming chores, you should surround yourself with images, colors, music, flavors, and fragrances that you will thereafter associate with the specific letter you are working on. These associations, of course, can be *anything*, but it is best if they have some vibratory connection to the letter, color, mood, or some quality or emotion attached to the letter.

For example, while working on Aleph, you can chew *Juicy Fruit®* gum and scent the room with a light incense, or with fresh lemon (for the yellow color), and repeatedly play light and airy (perhaps flute or harp) musical recordings. You can open a window or turn on a fan.

For Mem, you could munch blueberries and repeatedly play a favorite recording of Debussy's *La Mer* or Gershwin's *Rhapsody in Blue*.

For Shin, you could suck red hot cinnamon candy and play selections from Bizet's *Carmen*, etc.

Whatever you choose, make it simple, strong, memorable, and repetitive. It is even a good thing if you start to feel a little *overexposed* to these things while you are working. The stronger the sense-memory you associate with the letters, the more completely you will have installed them.

Pitch Pipe

Each letter of the Hebrew alphabet represents a specific layer or level of universal consciousness, which is reflected in the natural vibratory harmonies of all existence, including the frequencies of light and color. At various times during the First-Degree Initiation Ceremony, the movements and the actions that you and the officers made were accompanied by specific musical notes played by our talented (but unseen) Musician. Linking of the Hebrew letters with their specific musical notes is a technique intended to affect you *subconsciously* and trigger within your psyche a subliminal resonance to those specific frequencies of consciousness.

In your daily practices and meditations, however, we want you to go out of your way to *consciously* attune yourself with these specific notes. To help you do this, we are pleased to present you with a quality *pitch pipe*[5] for you to use in the various exercises in your First-Degree Portfolio. Of course, if you are a musician or have an organ or other electronic musical device in your home, this pitch pipe will be unnecessary. ·

Your First-Degree Home Temple

Now that you are a First-Degree Initiate, you are encouraged to set up your own First-Degree Temple. Actually . . . your real Temple is your own *body* . . . wait . . . *actually* your Temple is your own *soul* . . . wait . . . that's not right either . . . your real Temple is actually *you*. But, as you were told in your initiation, you probably aren't yet awake enough to realize the truth in what I'm saying. So, until you wake up, it's going to be helpful for you to set up and work in a Temple space you create for yourself in the comfort and privacy of your own home.

Sound like fun? It is!

Theoretically, your Temple is a symbolic miniature of the Temple in which you were initiated. But you won't need a whole house or building for your Temple. You won't even need a separate room (although that would be very cool). You just need a little dedicated space on the floor somewhere for you to place your *Altar*.

Your First-Degree Altar

Of course, you can get as fancy as you want with your Altar (after all, you're a Qabalah artist and can go as wild as your sense of art dictates!), but it doesn't need to be a big, expensive piece of furniture. A piece of wood raised from the floor by a few bricks and then covered with a beautiful cloth would work just fine for a First-Degree Altar. It only needs to be stable because it will serve both as your *Altar of Incense* and your *Altar of Light*. As you will probably be doing much of your meditation practices while sitting on or near the floor, a low Altar would work beautifully.

Be creative and have fun decorating your Altar. At the very least, it should be able to support the candelabra and an incense burner.

Setup Suggestions

Everything comprising your Temple setup should be suggestive of your degree and your initiatory experience. In the case of a First-Degree Temple, all that you see, hear, smell, or touch should bring to mind some quality or aspect of the number three and the Three Mother Letters.

Your Temple should be illuminated by a three-stemmed candelabra (with bright pale yellow, deep blue, and glowing orange-scarlet candles). Your Altar cloth and other hangings could be yellow, blue, and red. Incense should be chosen to be suggestive of primal Air, Water, or Fire. The three Hebrew letters themselves should also be visible. Perhaps some Tarot art . . . The Fool, Hanged Man, and Judgment, etc. Once you start thinking about these things, the artist in you will get all sorts of ideas; you'll start seeing threes *everywhere*. Soon your First-Degree Temple will expand to become the entire world around you!

EXERCISES AND MEDITATIONS

These are a few exercises, meditations, and practices recommended for you as a First-Degree Initiate. They are designed to attune you to the specific agencies and powers of consciousness associated with the Three Mother Letters of the Hebrew alphabet. The exercises are not difficult and do not require a great deal of time to execute. It is hoped that you will establish a reasonable daily routine and will be diligent in following it for a period of *ninety days.*

These exercises should be accompanied and enhanced (whenever possible and practical) by the appropriate incense or scents (even flavored gum or candies); music and temple colors will trigger to your mind memories of the specific letter or letters being worked.

Once you have mastered these preliminary exercises, you are encouraged to design your rituals and practices based on your expanding appreciation of the mysteries of the Three Mother Letters.

∴

SIMPLE HOME TEMPLE OPENING

*[To be performed prior to other home
rituals, exercises, or meditations.]*

[Sit before the Altar. Candles are unlit.]

[Clap three times.]

I dwell in *timelessness* before the birth of Creation.

I am poised at the *Formless Primal Center of Creation Yet-To-Be.*

I am the God that creates limitless space from my dimensionless center. I am the God that brings forth *form* from formlessness. I am the God that fashions *time* from timelessness.

I rule through the agency of the *Three Mother Letters*. *Three* extends and creates Space, Form, and Time, and in doing so casts a spell of illusion.

[Lighting the bright pale yellow Aleph candle]

Aleph extends, creating the Illusion of Above and Below.

[Lighting the deep blue Mem candle]

Mem extends, creating the Illusion of East and West.

[Lighting the glowing orange-scarlet Shin candle]

Shin extends, creating the Illusion of North and South.

[Make the First-Degree Sign[6] while intoning "A M Sh."]

The Light is extended. Temple is builded.

[Clap three times.]

The Temple is open.

∴

AMSH WARM-UP EXERCISE
[Done either standing or seated.]

1. Blow E note on the pitch pipe. Take a deep breath. Then sing as loud and as forcefully as possible until lungs are empty: **"Ahhhhhhhhhhhh."** Repeat three times while visualizing a beam of bright pale yellow light extending upward and downward from your heart.

2. Blow G# note on the pitch pipe. Take a deep breath. Then sing as loud and as forcefully as possible until lungs are empty: **"Mmmmmmmmmmmm."** Repeat three times while visualizing a beam of deep blue light extending to the right and to the left from your heart.

3. Blow C note on the pitch pipe. Take a deep breath. Then sing as loud and as forcefully as possible until lungs are empty: **"Sheeeeeeeeeee."** Repeat three times while visualizing a beam of glowing orange-scarlet light extending forward and backward from your heart.

Done correctly, this exercise should induce a noticeable feeling of warm euphoria. Close your eyes, and for a few moments enjoy the feeling while you visualize the three colored lines that create dimensional space radiating out from your heart.

More advanced variations can be developed incorporating the AMSh hand and body gestures made by the Worthy Guide during the First-Degree Opening ceremony and the *Touch of Awakening*.

∴

DAWN[7] AMSH BREATH CYCLE[8]

Sit comfortably in a chair or your accustomed meditation posture. Begin by taking three cleansing breaths.

Take a deep breath through the nose and hold for a moment. The full twelve-step cycle then begins:

1. Open the mouth and *exhale* slowly (emptying the lungs) while quietly whispering, **"Ahhhhhhhhhhh."**

2. Hold for a moment with the lungs empty.

3. Close the lips and *inhale* slowly (filling the lungs) while quietly whispering, **"Mmmmmmmmmmmm."**

4. Hold for a moment with the lungs full.

5. Open the lips and *exhale* slowly (emptying the lungs) while quietly whispering the hissing sound, **"Shhhhhhhhhhh."**

6. Hold for a moment with lungs empty.

7. Open the mouth and *inhale* slowly (filling the lungs) while quietly whispering, **"Ahhhhhhhhhhh."**

8. Hold for a moment with the lungs full.

9. Close the lips and *exhale* slowly (emptying the lungs) while quietly whispering, **"Mmmmmmmmmmmm."**

10. Hold for a moment with the lungs empty.

11. Open the lips and *inhale* slowly (filling the lungs) while whispering the hissing sound, **"Shhhhhhhhhhh."**

12. Hold for a moment with the lungs full.

END OF FIRST CYCLE

For the first few days, try to do ten cycles. The process will soon become automatic, pleasant, and relaxing. As you get better and you become increasingly relaxed, you will probably wish to lengthen the time you hold your breath in and out.

When the AMSh cycle becomes automatic, add the following color visualizations to the process:

∴

1. Open the mouth and exhale slowly (emptying the lungs) while quietly whispering, **"Ahhhhhhhhhhh."**

    - Fill the screen of your mind's eye with bright pale yellow.

2. Hold for a moment with the lungs empty.

    - Feel the totality of the bright pale yellow completely enveloping you, infusing every cell of your body.

3. Close the lips and inhale slowly (filling the lungs) while quietly whispering, **"Mmmmmmmmmmmmm."**

    - Fill the screen of your mind's eye with deep blue.

4. Hold for a moment with the lungs full.

    - Feel the totality of the deep blue completely enveloping you, infusing every cell of your body.

5. Open the mouth and exhale slowly (emptying the lungs) while quietly whispering the hissing sound, **"Shhhhhhhhhhh."**

    - Fill the screen of your mind's eye with glowing orange scarlet.

6. Hold for a moment with lungs empty.

    - Feel the totality of the glowing orange scarlet completely enveloping you, infusing every cell of your body.

7. Open the mouth and inhale slowly (filling the lungs) while quietly whispering, **"Ahhhhhhhhhhh."**

    - Fill the screen of your mind's eye with bright pale yellow.

8. Hold for a moment with the lungs full.

    - Feel the totality of the bright pale yellow completely enveloping you, infusing every cell of your body.

9. Close the lips and exhale slowly (emptying the lungs) while quietly whispering, **"Mmmmmmmmmmmmm."**

    - Fill the screen of your mind's eye with deep blue.

10. Hold for a moment with the lungs empty.

    - Feel the totality of the deep blue completely enveloping you, infusing every cell of your body.

11. Open the lips and inhale slowly (filling the lungs) while whispering the hissing sound, **"Shhhhhhhhhhh."**

    - Fill the screen of your mind's eye with glowing orange scarlet.

12. Hold for a moment with the lungs full.

    - Feel the totality of the glowing orange scarlet completely enveloping you, infusing every cell of your body.

End this exercise by filling the screen of your mind with pure black and feeling the peaceful totality of black enveloping you, infusing every cell of your body. Sit quietly in the empty blackness. Then record your thoughts and impressions in your journal.

∴

PASSING THE PYLONS
Astral Projection[9] into the World of the Three Mother Letters

While you're eating dinner, symbols are symbols—and living things are living things. While you're in a vision (or dying), symbols are living things—and living things are symbols.[10]

The purpose of this exercise is to attune and acclimate your psychic body[11] to the particular frequency of consciousness (Qabalistic Intelligence) exemplified by each letter. This is done by the technique of skrying[12] (or traveling in vision)—projecting your consciousness through the gateway[13] of the color-polarized floating ghost image of the letter itself, and then observing in vision the conditions of its unique "world." The details of these visions are unique to each individual. Nobody else can possibly interpret them for you because your visions are delivered through your own personal vocabulary of symbols and metaphors.

Once you become accustomed to the technique, you should then start to take control of the experience and become a proactive character in your own visionary adventure. Then things get interesting, and the mysteries of the letters begin to unfold as they can only unfold for you. Ride on wings of angels, soar through the heavens, let dragons swallow you, and see what's inside.

[Note:] It is vitally important to record the results of each and every skrying session in your journal. No matter how insignificant, silly, or embarrassing your visions, impressions, musings, mind wanderings, or daydreams may be, they are for the moment the impressions your psychic equipment is attuned to see at that vibratory level of consciousness. With practice, you will become better attuned to (and better able to interpret) the realities of that level.

[Another Note:] Try to "bring back" from every skrying session one symbol or image that you can at least temporarily associate with that world. Draw this symbol in your journal next to its Hebrew letter. Here's why. In the objective world of everyday consciousness, living things are living things, and symbols are symbols. But on the vision plane, it's not like that— there *symbols* (geometric figures, signs, logos, doodles) are *living things*. Conversely, *living things* (dragons, lions, angels, aardvarks) in visions are *symbols* of more complex and intangible qualities, hopes, fears, and so on.

So, when you bring a symbol back from your vision, you are literally importing a living spiritual being into your sleepy world of objective reality. Treat it with respect, and use it as a key when you reenter that plane during your next session.

Materials Needed:

- Pitch pipe

- Flash cards of Three Mother Letters

    ○ Bright pale yellow *Aleph*

    ○ Deep blue *Mem*

    ○ Glowing orange-scarlet *Shin*

- Blank white card

- Bright light

∴

PASSING THE PYLONS
Skrying Exercise

Example: Aleph

1. Carefully mount your blank white flash card at the *center right* of your Altar; and directly beside it (at the *center left* of the Altar) mount your bright pale yellow Aleph flash card.

2. Shine a bright light in such a way that it vibrantly illuminates both cards but does not shine into your eyes.

3. Comfortably seat yourself as near as possible to the two cards so that when you gaze at the letter, it essentially fills your field of vision.

4. Take your pitch pipe, find the E note, and blow.

5. Take a deep breath and forcefully sing, "Ahhhhhhhhhhh." *(Repeat three times.)*

6. Relax and gaze at the brightly illuminated bright pale yellow Aleph. Keep staring at the letter until it starts to do strange things.[14]

7. Then quickly turn your gaze to the plain white blank card.

   a. You should see a *pale mauve* Aleph floating over the white card. That ghost image is your gateway—your pylon.

   b. If you close your eyes and wait for a moment, the *pale mauve* ghost Aleph will clearly appear on the screen of your inner eyelids and remain floating for several seconds. If this doesn't happen, repeat steps 6 and 7 until it does.

8. When you have mastered the art of creating the ghost image of the letter on the screen of your closed eyes, you'll be ready to project your consciousness through the pylon and enter in vision the "world" of the letter.

9. The moment the ghost image is firmly visible on your closed eyes, make the First-Degree Sign[15] and whisper, "Ahhhhhhh-Mmmmmmmm-Shhhhhhh." Imagine yourself passing through the *pale mauve* Aleph as if it were a letter-shaped puff of smoke.

10. Now, just relax and let your mind and imagination wander wherever they want to go. There are no right or wrong things to see or think about. For a few minutes, you need only be the observer of your own vision. Whatever it is—whether it makes any sense to you or not—it is your vision for this session.

11. When you sense you have "seen" enough for this session, use your imagination to pass back into your Temple by again giving the First-Degree Sign and Word. Then open your eyes and clap three times.

12. Remember what I said earlier about journaling. Immediately record the details of *everything* you saw or everything you thought about during the skrying session. Don't omit anything, no matter how insignificant you might think it is. Your only goal (at first) is to bring back one symbol. You will analyze it later.

You may at first have difficulty learning how to be the observer of your own daydream-like visions, but you *will* soon get the hang of it. When you finally do, you will realize that you were doing it all along and the trick was simply to shift your center of consciousness from the *you* sitting in front of the Altar to the *you* that passed through the pylon.

Aleph

Image on card:	Bright Pale Yellow Aleph
Pitch pipe note:	E
Word sung:	Ahhhhhh
Ghost Aleph:	Pale Mauve

The procedure for the two other Mother Letters (Mem and Shin) is exactly as in the Aleph example above. The only differences are shown here:

Mem

Image on card:	Dark Blue Mem
Pitch pipe note:	G#
Word sung:	Mmmmmmmm
Ghost Mem:	Bright Orange

Shin

Image on card: Glowing Orange Scarlet Shin
Pitch pipe note: C
Word sung: Shhhhhhh
Ghost Shin: Emerald Green

SECOND-DEGREE
INTRODUCTORY WORDS

By Lon Milo DuQuette

The Number Seven seals the limits of Space and Form and Time; and by doing so divides itself against itself to become the God of opposing forces, qualities, and appearances—a God who sleeps and dreams it opposes a devil; a light that sleeps and dreams it opposes darkness.

Ideally, the Second-Degree ceremony is conferred upon one candidate per occasion. It focuses on the mysteries of the development (or devolution) of consciousness expressed by the Seven Double Letters of the Hebrew alphabet. It is not as long as the First-Degree ceremony and utilizes more music and projected image cues. The ceremony also features an elaborately illustrated floorcloth or symbolic carpet (fully described and illustrated in the script), such as is commonly used by other mystical and fraternal organizations.

It is clear by the notes that accompanied the scripts that Second-Degrees were also held at hotel venues.

SECOND-DEGREE
PRELIMINARY NOTES

This version of the script is written assuming the Candidate is male.[1] Those wishing to perform or exemplify this ritual are encouraged to make all changes necessary to accommodate any gender identification.

It is preferred (though not absolutely necessary) that the Second-Degree Initiation be conferred in its entirety for one Candidate at a time. Ideally, the ceremony is scheduled no sooner than three months (ninety days) following the First-Degree Initiation.

The Candidate must verbally affirm his or her familiarity with the First-Degree Study Material, but no formal examination or proficiency test is administered.

IMPORTANT NOTE ON SAFETY:

O∴ H∴ O∴ initiations should never (at any time before, during, or after the ceremony) be the occasion to frighten, belittle, or humiliate the Candidate, who at all times shall be treated with the utmost courtesy and respect.

PRELUDE TO THE SECOND-DEGREE INITIATION CEREMONY
Officer's Script

[The officers are the same as in the First-Degree ceremony, and the Temple is at first arranged exactly as for a First-Degree Initiation.]

[The Temple is ceremonially opened in the First-Degree.][2]

[The Candidate for the Second-Degree is present in the Temple during the First-Degree Opening. He stands in the center of the Temple west of HT's chair.]

[The First-Degree Opening concludes when HT says . . .]

HT: *[Claps three times.]*
The Sign is made. The Grip is given. The Word is Spoken. I declare the Temple open in the First-Degree.

> *[HT is seated. Candidate and WG remain standing.]*

HT: *[Claps 3-1-3.]*
Worthy Guide, assist me now to open the *Temple of the Seven*. Satisfy yourself that all present are *Second-Degree* Initiates.

WG: *[Turns and loudly addresses the Candidate.]*
Let all present stand to order and present themselves as Second-Degree Initiates of Our Holy Order. You will give me the *Sign* of the Second-Degree.

> *[There is a pause while the Candidate, obviously confused*
> *and unable to give the Sign, fails to comply.]*

WG: *[Turns and addresses HT.]*
Honored Teacher, I have discovered there is a *Master of the Three Letters* present among us, but he has failed to demonstrate the proper Tokens that would prove his worthiness to join us in our work in the *Temple of Seven*. It is obvious he has not yet attained balance, nor has he been tempered by the *Ordeal of the Seven Double Letters.*

HT:
Worthy Guide, do not be quick to condemn our Brother's motives. Perhaps his aspirations are pure. *(addressing Candidate)* Friend and Comrade, your awkward intrusion upon our sacred work suggests to us that your continued attraction to our mysteries might be an omen of great significance. Is it truly your will to advance to the Second-Degree of Our Holy Order?

CANDIDATE:
Yes.

HT:
While I admire your courage and audacity, I must warn you that in order to successfully penetrate our mysteries, you must first attain *balance* and be *tempered* by the *Ordeal of the Seven Letters*. Are you willing to submit yourself to such an ordeal?

CANDIDATE:
Yes.

HT: *[Cont.]*
Then, your will be done! I direct the Worthy Guide to escort you to a place of solitude and quiet reflection. In your meditations, search deep in your heart and ruthlessly root out and banish any and all demons of *duality* and *imbalance* that haunt the recesses of your soul. Be diligent in your search.

For should you not banish these devils *before* you again enter our Temple, they will surely tear you asunder *after* you enter.

> *[WG escorts the Candidate out of the*
> *Temple to the waiting area.]*[3]

> *[WG returns to the Temple and assists HT in*
> *rearranging the room for the Second-Degree*
> *Opening and Initiation Ceremonies.]*

O ∴ H ∴ O ∴

Our Holy Order
CEREMONY OF INITIATION
SECOND-DEGREE
Officer's Script

Figure 5.

OFFICERS

(Officers are the same as in the Ceremony of the First-Degree.)

Sign, Grip, and Word of the Second-Degree

The Second-Degree *Sign* is given as follows:

- First, raise both hands to the side of the head (palms turned backward).
- Then holding the pinkies down with the thumbs, extend three remaining fingers (as a child might indicate the number three).
- Then drop both hands to the side of the body.
- Finally, join the tips of the thumbs and forefingers to form an upright triangle with the hands.
- Place the triangle over the Third Eye area of the forehead.

The Second-Degree *Grip* is given as follows:

- First, give the First-Degree Grip.
- Then each place the four fingers of the left hand on the right wrist.

The Second-Degree *Word* is "Menorah" and is exchanged in three parts as follows:

- The first says, "MEN."
- The second responds, "OR."
- The first responds, "AH."
- Together they say, "MEN-OR-AH."

Miscellaneous items to have on hand for the ceremony:

- For each Candidate:
  - Cube Toy of Seven Letters
  - Second-Degree Study Portfolio

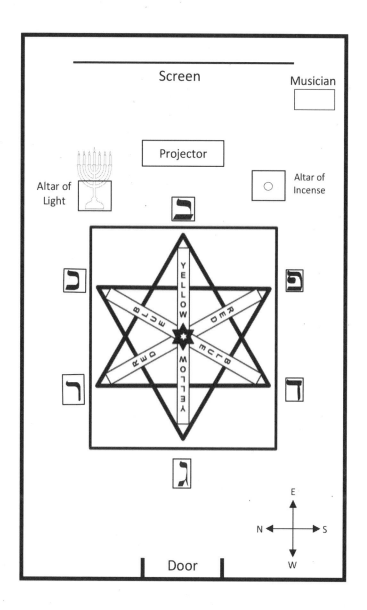

FIGURE 6. SECOND-DEGREE TEMPLE WITH FLOORCLOTH.

- For the Second-Degree Temple, all chairs from the First-Degree Temple (including the *Chair of the Honored Teacher*) are removed from the room. (Three cushions for Part III are concealed until needed.) Until the third section, Officers and Candidate stand throughout.

- As in the First-Degree Temple, a large projection screen is set up in the East, and a projector rests on a small table in front of the screen at an appropriate distance to project images on the screen.

- The *Musician's station* remains concealed South of the screen. (*Musician*, being concealed, may, of course, remain seated.) As in the First-Degree, musical and tonal cues will again be played during certain sections of the ceremony. The organ (or electronic device) and the remote-control device for the projector are concealed in a place convenient for Musician to operate.

- The *Altar of Incense*, upon which rests a censer of smoking frankincense or other sweet-smelling resinous wood gum, remains in the South. (The *Altar of Incense* may need to be moved slightly from its precise First-Degree position to accommodate the Second-Degree *floorcloth*.)

- The *Altar of Light* remains in the North. (The *Altar of Light* may also need to be moved slightly from its precise First-Degree position to accommodate the Second-Degree *floorcloth*.)

- The three-candle *candelabra* (that was used in the First-Degree) is removed and replaced with a *seven-branched Menorah*.

NOTE CONCERNING THE MENORAH:

The Menorah plays a very important role in the Second-Degree Initiation. It must be lightweight, so as to be easily carried about the Temple by an Officer. It must be the traditional design with a central stem flanked by three stems on both sides. (See Figure 7.) Six candles are inserted on the six ends of three semicircular arms plus one candle on the central stem. (This is a very common design for inexpensive home and decorative Menorahs.) The seven candles represent the *Seven Double Letters* of the Hebrew alphabet, and they are colored to represent the seven Planetary Spheres represented by the letters. When one is facing the Menorah, they are arranged thusly:

FIGURE 7. SECOND-DEGREE MENORAH.

"*. . . three are against three, and one places them in equilibrium.*"

—*Sepher Yezirah*, VI: VII.

- On the center stem, the *black* candle for *Tav* and *Saturn*.

- On the two ends of the topmost semicircular arm (the two candles to the left and right of the center black candle)—*yellow* candle for *Beth* and the sphere of *Mercury*, and *blue* candle for *Gimel* and the sphere of *Luna*.

- On the two ends of the middle semicircular arm (the two candles to the left and right of the yellow and blue candles)—*emerald green* candle for *Daleth* and the sphere of *Venus*, and *violet* candle for *Kaph* and the sphere of *Jupiter*.

- On the two ends of the lowest semicircular arm (the two candles to the left and right of the green and violet candles)—*scarlet* candle for *Peh* and the sphere of *Mars*, and *orange* candle for *Resh* and the sphere of *Sol*.

  To a person facing the Menorah, the order of the seven candles is (from left to right): scarlet, emerald green, yellow, black (as the central candle), blue, violet, and orange.

NOTES CONCERNING THE FLOORCLOTH:

The *floorcloth* plays a very important role in the Second-Degree Initiation.[1] (See Figure 8.) It is a rectangular carpet (approximately 7 by 7½ feet) made of canvas, oilcloth, linen, or any convenient cloth material of substantial thickness; and painted with the hexagram design shown in the figure.[2] The background of the floorcloth is white or a light, neutral tone. The three central beams are brightly painted—yellow (for Aleph), blue (for Mem), and red (for Shin).

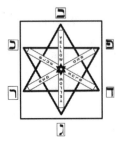

FIGURE 8. SECOND-DEGREE FLOORCLOTH.

During the ceremony, the Candidate will be required to physically maintain his *balance* as he carefully treads the length of each of the three central beams. This "ordeal" is meant to be slightly difficult to accomplish, as the beams are rather narrow. But it is important that the Candidate forge a psychic and physiological association within himself that permanently links the physical *ordeal* of maintaining his balance with the paradoxical *meanings* of the Seven Letters of this degree. If the Candidate's foot should step over the outline of a beam at any time, he will be asked to begin again. It must take concentration and a concerted effort on the part of the Candidate to maintain his *balance* throughout the simple ordeal.

IMPORTANT NOTE CONCERNING TEMPLE DIRECTIONS REFERRED TO IN INITIATION SCRIPT:

Do not be confused about directions that are referred to in the initiation script.

- There are "stage" directions (e.g., "southeast," "northeast," "southwest," "southeast"), which refer to the physical coordinates within the Temple room itself. These are necessary for the officers to know how to move about the Temple. The stage directions are referenced using the small compass image in the lower right of the Temple diagram. In the script, stage directions always appear *uncapitalized* in the bracketed and italicized notes.

- And there are the six *Qabalistic* directions (i.e., "Above," "Below," "East," "West," "North," "South") that refer to the cosmic directions attributed to the Hebrew letters. In the script, these directions always appear *capitalized* in the dialog of the initiation script itself.

I

OPENING CEREMONY

[The Temple, having been properly rearranged for the Second-Degree, is now completely dark.]

[WG goes to the Altar of Incense and ignites the charcoal.]

HT: *[Claps 3-1-3.]*
How peaceful and profound is this Darkness absolute. It swallows up even the thought of darkness and light.

[HT goes to the Altar of Light and lights the Black Saturn candle in the center of the Menorah. The Temple is now, for the moment, lit only by this candle.]

HT: *[Claps 3-1-3.]*
Worthy Guide, what is the hour?

WG:
Honored Teacher, it is the silent, dark moment before Light expands and shatters into vibrations of color and sound and shifting forms and pairs of opposites.

HT: *[Claps 3-1-3.]*
Worthy Guide, what is this place?

WG:
Light in Extension, Honored Teacher.

HT: *[Claps 3-1-3.]*
Worthy Guide, what is the source of *Light in Extension?*

WG:
Honored Teacher, it is hidden.

HT: *[Claps 3-1-3.]*
Worthy Guide, what God utters the Word that shatters the Light into vibrations of colors and sounds? What God speaks and seals the limits of Space and Form and Time?

WG:
The *Number Seven*, Honored Teacher—through the agency of the *Seven Double Letters* of the Hebrew alphabet. As it is written in the *Sepher Yezirah:*

> *There are seven, of which three are against three, and one places them in equilibrium.*[3]

The *Number Seven* seals the limits of Space and Form and Time, and by doing so divides itself *against* itself to become the God of opposing forces, qualities, and appearances—a God who sleeps and dreams it opposes a devil; a light that sleeps and dreams it opposes darkness.

HT:
But, Worthy Guide, is not this dream of the Number Seven the nature of all phenomena in the dimensional universe we perceive around us? Is it not the nature of objective reality?

WG:
Indeed it is, Honored Teacher, if we understand *reality* to be that which is perceived by someone who is also trapped in the same dream.

- *Seven* is *phantom Life* that dreams of *Death.*

- *Seven* is *phantom Peace* that dreams of *War.*

- *Seven* is *phantom Wisdom* that dreams of *Folly.*

- *Seven* is *phantom Wealth* that dreams of *Poverty.*

- *Seven* is *phantom Beauty* that dreams of *Ugliness.*

- *Seven* is *phantom Fruitfulness* that dreams of *Sterility.*

- *Seven* is *phantom Dominion* that dreams of *Slavery.*

HT: *[Claps 3-1-3.]*
Worthy Guide, what do we call this world of duality?

WG:
Honored Teacher, it is called the *Macrocosm*, the "Greater World" . . . for it casts a great spell—so great a spell the uninitiated believe the Macrocosm to be God and the cosmos, and the unawakened believe it to be Heaven.

HT:
What are the Seven Double Letters?

WG:
Beth and Gimel—Daleth and Kaph—Peh and Resh . . . and Tav.

HT:
And do these words have meaning?

WG:
Indeed, they do, Honored Teacher. Beth is a "House" and Gimel a "Camel"— Daleth a "Door" and Kaph the "Palm of a Hand"—Peh is the "Mouth" and Resh is the "Face" . . . and Tav is a "Cross" or a "Mark" that seals the gates of existence from within and without.

HT:
What are the duties of the Seven Double Letters?

WG:
- Beth and Gimel mount the Mother Letter *Aleph* and seal infinite Above and infinite Below;

- Daleth and Kaph mount the Mother Letter *Mem* and seal infinite East and infinite West;

- Peh and Resh mount the Mother Letter *Shin* and seal infinite North and infinite South.

HT:
And the Letter *Tav*? What position does Tav hold? What direction does Tav seal?

WG:
No position, Honored Teacher. No direction. Tav is the inscrutable source and center of the Macrocosm. From Tav burst the rays of the Three Mother Letters whose extension, in turn, creates Above/Below; East/West; North/South.

> *[HT faces WG. Both simultaneously give the Second-Degree Sign. They then exchange the Second-Degree Grip. They hold this gesture as they exchange the Second-Degree Word.]*

HT:
MEN-

WG:
OR-

HT:
AH.

HT & WG: *[Together]*
MENORAH.

HT:
The Sign is made. The Grip is given. The Word is Spoken. I declare the Temple open in the Second-Degree.

HT: *[Claps 3-1-3.]*
The Temple is builded. Worthy Guide, ascertain if our Master of the Three Letters is still determined to be Master of the Seven.

II

RECEPTION OF THE CANDIDATE

[The screen is BLACK and will remain so during this section.]

[There are many single-note musical cues for this section.][4]

[The Temple is lit only by the single Tav candle of the Menorah.]

*[At the beginning of the ceremony, HT stands at the center
of the floorcloth (at the junction of the three beams).]*

*[WG goes without and summons the Candidate and
guides him to a place just outside the Temple door.]*

WG: *[Speaking to Candidate in a soft yet solemn tone of voice]*
Is it your will to be received into the Mysteries of Our Holy Order in the
Second-Degree?

CANDIDATE:
Yes.

WG:
Then you must, of your own free will and accord, knock *seven times* upon
the door—three knocks; then one knock; then three knocks again.

[Done (knock 3-1-3).]

HT: *[Speaking loudly enough to be heard through the closed door]*
Who stands at the threshold of Macrocosm and boldly knocks as though he
were Master of the Seven Letters?

WG: *[Speaking loudly enough to be heard through the closed door]*
A Master of the Three Letters who desires to penetrate the Temple of the
Seven Double Letters.

HT: *[Speaking loudly enough to be heard through the closed door]*
Friend and Comrade, your audacity and persistence will earn for you both
blessing and curse. No one shall open this door for you! You must push it
open yourself! Enter if you dare!

*[Candidate opens the door and enters the Temple.
WG follows him in and closes the door. WG guides the
Candidate west of the floorcloth, facing the HT (who stands
in the center of the floorcloth facing the Candidate). The
Temple is very dark, being lit solely by the single black
(Tav) candle of the Menorah on the Altar of Light.]*

HT:
In the Beginning ...

*[As HT speaks, WG goes to the Altar of Light, picks up
the Menorah, and returns to the Candidate's side.]*

HT: *[Cont.]*

. . . the Earth was without form and void; and darkness was upon the face of the deep. And God said, "Let there be light . . . "

> *[WG pushes the Menorah close to Candidate's face*
> *and (as silently as possible) indicates he should pluck*
> *the black Tav candle from its stem. When Candidate*
> *is holding the lit candle, HT finishes his sentence.]*

HT: *[Cont.]*

" . . . . and there was light."

. . . .

MUSIC

A.[5]

. . . .

HT: *[Cont.]*

And God divided the light from the darkness.

> *[WG escorts the Candidate to the center of the floorcloth.]*

> *[HT applies the Touch of Awakening[6]*
> *(A M Sh) upon the Candidate.]*

> *[HT withdraws to east of the floorcloth and turns to*
> *face Candidate, who now stands alone in the center*
> *of the floorcloth holding the black candle of Tav.]*

HT:

Master of the Three Letters, look down and around you. You are poised as the source and center of all; from *you* radiate three beams representing the Three Mother Letters—Aleph, Mem, and Shin. These three rays extend ever outward from you, and in doing so create space itself. For the *Macrocosm* must have *space* in which to manifest.

> *[Move from center to Beth]*

HT:

Close your eyes for a moment and hear the fundamental vibration. Feel the boundless bliss of perfect equilibrium. Become one with *Tav*. As the *Formless Primal Center*, there is no limit to your *inwardness*—so too, there can be no limit to the *outwardness* of your Light.

Open your eyes and behold! As the light of your single candle instantly fills the immensity of the darkened Temple, so too does the light of Tav fashion expanding space and consciousness.

Tav in Hebrew means a "mark" or a "seal"—because Tav seals the limits of existence itself. Mount now the yellow beam of Aleph, and, maintaining your single-focused balance, bear your light eternally upward, and *seal* the infinite Above.

....

MUSIC

E.[7]

....

[As the Candidate walks the yellow beam, WG (holding the Menorah) takes HT's place (at the east end of the yellow Aleph beam) so that the Candidate approaches the WG.]

[In the meantime, HT moves to the opposite (west) end of the yellow Aleph beam.]

[Candidate reaches the top end of the yellow beam of Aleph and is stopped by WG, who holds the Menorah close to the Candidate's eyes.]

Music stops.

....

WG:

There is truly no end to Aleph's upward projection. See your light piercing on through the darkness before you. But our minds must set dream limits to infinites. So, we imagine that "Above" is sealed, like the ceiling of this room. Above is sealed by the letter *Beth.*

Seal now the eternal Above by lighting the yellow candle of *Beth.*

[Using the flame of the black Tav candle, the Candidate lights the yellow candle of Beth.]

....

MUSIC

High-E chime.[8]

....

WG:

Above is sealed and the light continues eternally upward. Turn now, and maintaining your perfect balance, return to the *Formless Primal Center* and stop.

....

MUSIC

E.[9]

....

[Candidate reaches center.]

....

MUSIC

Low A.[10]

....

[Move from center to Gimel]

HT:
Having sealed infinite "Above" and returned to the *Formless Primal Center*, continue on the yellow beam of Aleph, and, maintaining your single-focused balance, bear your light eternally downward and *seal* the infinite Below.

....

MUSIC

E.[11]

....

[As the Candidate walks the yellow beam, WG (holding the Menorah) takes HT's place (at the west end of the yellow beam of Aleph) so that the Candidate approaches the WG.]

[In the meantime, HT moves to the southwest end of the blue beam of Mem.]

[Candidate reaches the end (west) of the yellow beam of Aleph and is stopped by WG, who holds the Menorah close to the Candidate's eyes.]

Music stops.

....

WG:
There is truly no end to Aleph's downward projection, but our minds must set dream limits to infinites. So, we imagine that "Below" is sealed, like the floor of this room. Below is sealed by the letter *Gimel*.

Seal now the eternal Below by lighting the blue candle of *Gimel*.

[Using the flame of the black Tav candle, the Candidate lights the blue candle of Gimel.]

....

MUSIC

High G# chime.[12]

....

WG:
Below is sealed and the light continues eternally downward. You have fulfilled Aleph's sacred duty. Now turn, and maintaining your perfect balance, return to the *Formless Primal Center* and stop.

[The Candidate carefully turns on the yellow beam and walks back to the center.]

....

MUSIC

E.[13]

....

[Candidate reaches center.]

....

MUSIC

Low A.[14]

....

[Move from center to Daleth]

HT:

Tav, in Hebrew, means a "mark" or a "seal." Mount now the blue beam of Mem, and, maintaining your single-focused balance, bear your light eternally Eastward, and *seal* the infinite East.

....

MUSIC

$G^{\#}$.[15]

....

[As the Candidate walks the blue beam, WG (holding the Menorah) takes HT's place (at the southwest end of the blue beam of Mem) so that the Candidate approaches the WG.]

[In the meantime, HT moves to the opposite end of the blue beam of Mem in the northeast.]

[Candidate reaches the southwest end of the blue beam of Mem and is stopped by WG, who holds the Menorah close to the Candidate's eyes.]

Music stops.

....

WG:

There is truly no end to Mem's Eastward projection. See your light piercing on through the darkness before you. But our minds must set dream limits to infinites. So, we imagine that "East" is sealed, like a wall of this room. East is sealed by the letter *Daleth*. Seal now the eternal East by lighting the green candle of *Daleth*.

[Using the flame of the black Tav candle, the Candidate lights the green candle of Daleth.]

....

MUSIC

High-$F^{\#}$ chime.[16]

....

WG:

The East is sealed and the light continues eternally Eastward. Turn now, and, maintaining your perfect balance, return to the *Formless Primal Center* and stop.

....

MUSIC

$G^{\#}$.[17]

....

[Candidate reaches center.]

....

MUSIC

Low A.[18]

....

[Move from center to Kaph]

HT:

Having sealed the infinite "East" and returned to the *Formless Primal Center*, continue on the blue beam of Mem, and, maintaining your single-focused balance, bear your light eternally Westward and *seal* the infinite West.

....

MUSIC

$G^{\#}$.[19]

....

[As the Candidate walks the blue beam, WG (holding the Menorah) takes HT's place (at the northeast end of the blue Mem beam) so that the Candidate approaches the WG.]

[In the meantime, HT moves to the southeast end of the red beam of Shin.]

[Candidate reaches the end (northeast) of the blue beam of Mem and is stopped by WG, who holds the Menorah close to the Candidate's eyes.]

Music stops.

....

WG:

There is truly no end to Mem's Westward projection. See your light piercing on through the darkness before you. But our minds must set dream limits to infinites. So, we imagine that the "West" is sealed, like a wall of this room. West is sealed by the letter *Kaph*.

Seal now the eternal West by lighting the violet candle of *Kaph*.

[Using the flame of the black Tav candle, the Candidate lights the violet candle of Kaph.]

....

MUSIC

$B^{\flat}$ *chime.*[20]

....

WG:

The West is sealed and the light continues eternally Westward. You have fulfilled Mem's sacred duty. Now turn, and, maintaining your perfect balance, return to the *Formless Primal Center* and stop.

[The Candidate carefully turns on the blue beam and walks back to center.]

....

MUSIC

$G^{\#}.$[21]

....

[Candidate reaches center.]

....

MUSIC

$A.$[22]

....

[Move from center to Peh]

HT:

Tav, in Hebrew, means a "mark" or a "seal." Mount now the red beam of Shin, and, maintaining your single-focused balance, bear your light eternally Northward and *seal* the infinite North.

....

MUSIC

$C.$[23]

....

[As the Candidate walks the beam, WG (holding the Menorah) takes HT's place (at the southeast end of the red beam of Shin) so that the Candidate approaches the WG.]

[In the meantime, HT moves to the opposite end of the red Shin beam in the northwest.]

[Candidate reaches the southeast end of the red beam of Shin and is stopped by WG, who holds the Menorah close to the Candidate's eyes.]

Music stops.

....

WG:

There is truly no end to Shin's Northward projection. See your light piercing on through the darkness before you. But our minds must set dream limits to infinites. So, we imagine that "North" is sealed, like a wall of this room. North is sealed by the letter *Peh*.

Seal now the eternal North by lighting the scarlet candle of *Peh*.

*[Using the flame of the black Tav candle, the
Candidate lights the scarlet candle of Peh.]*

....

MUSIC

C chime.[24]

....

WG:

The North is sealed and the light continues eternally Northward. Turn now,
and, maintaining your perfect balance, return to *the Formless Primal Center*
and stop.

....

MUSIC

C.[25]

....

[Candidate reaches Center.]

....

MUSIC

Low A.[26]

....

[Move from center to Resh]

HT:

Having sealed the infinite "North" and returned to the *Formless Primal
Center*, continue on the red beam of Shin, and, maintaining your single-
focused balance, bear your light eternally Southward and *seal* the infinite
South.

....

MUSIC

C.[27]

....

*[As the Candidate walks the beam, WG (holding the
Menorah) takes HT's place (at the northwest end of the red
beam of Shin) so that the Candidate approaches the WG.]*

[In the meantime, HT moves to the east of the floorcloth.]

*[Candidate reaches the other end (northwest) of the
red beam of Shin and is stopped by WG, who holds
the Menorah close to the Candidate's eyes.]*

Music stops.

....

WG:

There is truly no end to Shin's Southward projection. See your light piercing on through the darkness before you. But our minds must set dream limits to infinites. So, we imagine that the "South" is sealed, like a wall of this room. South is sealed by the letter *Resh*.

Seal now the eternal South by lighting the orange candle of *Resh*.

> *[Using the flame of the black Tav candle, the
> Candidate lights the orange candle of Resh.]*

MUSIC

High-D chime.[28]

WG:

The South is sealed and the light continues eternally Southward. You have fulfilled Shin's sacred duty. Now turn, and, maintaining your perfect balance, return to the *Formless Primal Center* and stop.

> *[The Candidate carefully turns on the red
> beam and walks back to center.]*

MUSIC

C.[29]

> *[Candidate reaches the center.]*

MUSIC

Low A.[30]

> *[HT approaches the Candidate from the east to apply
> the "Touch of the Breaking of the Seven Seals."]*

HT:

Having sealed the six directions of space, you stand again in perfect equilibrium at the central seventh. Break now the Seven Seals.

HT: *[Using his **left** thumb, touches Candidate's **right** ear and says]*
Beth.

HT: *[Using his **right** thumb, touches Candidate's **left** ear and says]*
Gimel.

HT: *[Leaving thumb in place and using his **left** index finger, touches slightly behind Candidate's **right** ear and says]*
Daleth.

HT: *[Leaving thumb in place and using his **right** index finger, touches slightly behind Candidate's **left** temple and says]*
Kaph.

HT: *[Leaving thumb and index finger in place, using his **left** middle finger, touches just to the right side of Candidate's brain stem and says]*
Peh.

HT: *[Leaving thumb and index finger in place, using his **right** middle finger, touches just to the left side of Candidate's brain stem and says]*
Resh. . . . "Three against three."

HT: *[Joining the tips of his thumbs and forefingers to form an upright triangle with his hands, "crowns" the Candidate's forehead with the triangle and says]*
Tav. . . . "and one places them in equilibrium."

> *[Secretly using the Grip of the Second-Degree, HT shakes the hand of the Candidate and says]*

HT:
Friend and Comrade, welcome to the Temple of the Seven Letters of Our Holy Order. But before you are truly *Master of the Seven Double Letters*, you must be tempered by the Ordeal of the Seven.

For the moment, however, I observe that you will appreciate a short pause in the formalities so that you may refresh yourself and gather your strength for the challenges that await you. Worthy Guide will now escort you from the Temple to a place of rest and refreshment. Upon your return, I will communicate to you the secret keys that unlock the mysteries of this degree; after which, we shall proceed with our work.

> *[WG escorts Candidates to the waiting area and bids them to quietly relax for a few minutes and enjoy water and light refreshments.]*

> *[Meanwhile, HT places three cushions on the floorcloth in preparation for the Ordeal of the Seven Letters.]*

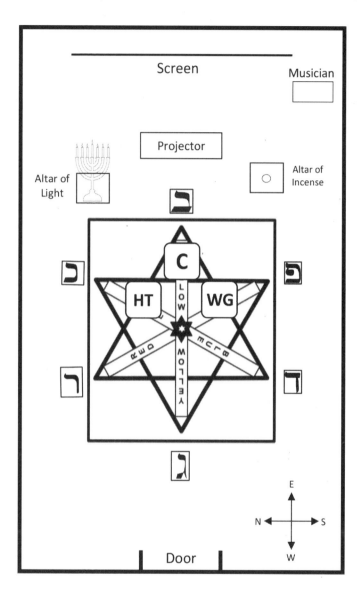

FIGURE 9. CUSHION POSITIONS ON FLOORCLOTH.

III

PENETRATION OF THE TEMPLE OF THE SEVEN DOUBLE LETTERS

*[There are many musical and projector cues
for this section of the ceremony.]*

*[WG collects the Candidate in the waiting area and guides
him to the outside of the Temple door (which is closed). WG
instructs the Candidate to knock loudly seven times.]*

[Done (knocks 3-1-3).]

[HT goes to the door. He does not yet open it.]

HT: *[Speaking loudly from inside the Temple door]*
Who knocks at the door of the Temple of the Seven Double Letters?

WG: *[Loudly answers from outside the Temple door]*
A Dear Friend and Comrade who has broken the Seven Seals and has been
duly received in Our Holy Order, and now demands entrance to the *Temple
of the Seven Double Letters* to be tempered by the Ordeal of the Seven.

HT: *[From inside the Temple door]*
Does he volunteer of his own free will and accord to undergo such an
ordeal?

*[Even if the Candidate has heard the question,
WG carefully repeats question.]*

WG: *[To Candidate]*
Do you volunteer of your own free will and accord to undergo such an
ordeal?

*[If Candidate agrees, WG encourages
him to loudly answer, "Yes."]*

CANDIDATE: *[From outside the Temple door]*
YES!

*[Hearing the Candidate's affirmative answer,
HT opens the door and greets Candidate at the
threshold with a warm and loving smile.]*

HT:
I greet you at the threshold of the *Temple of the Seven Double Letters*! However, before you can penetrate the membrane of our sacred Temple, you must prove to us that you have broken the Seven Seals. Worthy Guide, please instruct our Comrade how to properly give the *Sign*, *Grip*, and *Word* of the Second-Degree.

WG: *[Demonstrating for Candidate]*
The Second-Degree *Sign* is given as follows:

- First, raise both hands to the side of the head (palms turned backwards).

- Then holding the pinkies down with the thumbs, extend three remaining fingers (as a child might indicate the number three).

- Then drop both hands to the side of the body.

- Finally, join the tips of the thumbs and forefingers to form an upright triangle with the hands.

- Place the triangle over the Third Eye area of the forehead.

[Candidate repeats action.]

WG: *[Cont.]*
The Second-Degree *Grip* is given as follows:

- First, give the First-Degree Grip.

- Then each place the four fingers of the left hand on the right wrist.

[WG exchanges Grip with Candidate.]

The Second-Degree *Word* is *Menorah* and is exchanged in three parts as follows:

- The first says, "MEN."

- The second responds, "OR."

- The first responds, "AH."

- Together they say, "MEN-OR-AH."

[WG exchanges Word with Candidate.]

HT:

Dear Friend and Comrade, these are the Signs and Tokens whereby one Second-Degree initiate of Our Holy Order may know another. These actions may appear on the surface to be childish and whimsical. I assure you, however, the magical significance of these simple gestures and words is profound and powerful. Memorize them. Meditate upon them. You must prove proficient in their execution in order to gain admission to a Second-Degree Temple.

But more importantly, you most assuredly will be called upon to employ them as magic gestures that serve to open doors and unlock mysterious levels of consciousness in your own dreams and astral visions. They are in truth the secret Signs and Words that open up the next level of your own awakening.

I now invite you to take your seat in the Temple.

*[HT and WG escort Candidate to his cushion on
the floorcloth and instruct him to be seated so he
may comfortably view the screen in the East.]*

*[HT and WG seat themselves in back and to each side of
the Candidate so they can speak unseen into his ears.]*

*[The Musician's role during this section is very important
and must be synchronized precisely to the changes of images
on the screen. These changes are a vitally important aspect to
the ritual because of the effects they are designed to have on the
Candidate's consciousness. All care must be taken to ensure the
Candidate experience the "floating ghost" optical phenomena
of Hebrew letters at the proper moment in the ceremony.]*[31]

....

MUSIC

Mid-range E held.

....

בּ [Heb: Beth]

....

SLIDE # ?[32]

Large yellow Beth against blue background.

....

HT:

Behold the Sacred Letter *Beth*. With the light of Beth, you sealed the infinite Above. With the light of Beth, the sphere of *Mercury* was created in the Macrocosm. Gaze intently upon the letter *Beth* and perhaps you will hear the voice of the god Mercury speak to your soul.

[Pause.]

HT: *[As Mercury]*
I am Mercury, Messenger of the Gods. I am the God of Intellect and Logic, Divination, Financial Gain, Language, and Eloquence of Speech. Why do you come to me?

WG: *[For Candidate, who repeats]*
It is my will to awaken to perfect realization of myself. I cannot awaken to perfection until I have balanced within my soul the Blessings and the Curses of Mercury and Beth.

HT: *[As Mercury]*
You are wise and very brave to make such a fearsome request. It is true. When you awaken to my light, I freely pour my treasures upon you. A Rich Harvest of Delight is yours. Life, Wisdom. Genius, Learning. Brilliance of Wit, Eloquence of Tongue, and the Power to Heal the Sicknesses of Men and Women. These gifts are yours.

[Pause.]

....

SLIDE # ?

Large blue Beth against yellow background.

....

HT: *[As Mercury, Cont.]*
But beware! My Light is so pure, it is one with my Shadow, and my Shadow, when he stands alone, is a great sorcerer. HE will deceive you. He brings *Death*. He rots your mind with madness and confusion. He transforms all your truths into lies. He corrupts the Splendor of your accomplishments and steals away the health of your body and soul . . . if you fall under his Spell. Do NOT look upon HIM!

....

SLIDE # ?

Total blackness.

....

[Pause.]

....

SLIDE # ?

Large yellow Hebrew Beth against blue background.

....

WG:
Gaze deeply at the Sacred Letter *Beth*. To the unawakened, it is the letter of *Life and Death*. Don't take your eyes from it.

....

*Slide changes to bright white; in doing so, creates the floating
blue ghost image of Beth in the Candidate's brain.*

....

HT:

See now, with the eyes of your soul, the true color and image of Beth. Close
your eyes and implant it deep in the center of your brain.

[Pause.]

I now bless you. But be ever mindful that the Blessings of Mercury and
Beth are a Curse; and the Curses of Mercury and Beth are a Blessing.
You will know you have truly awakened when you see neither Curse nor
Blessing.

....

SLIDE # ?

Total blackness.

....

MUSIC

Mid-range G♯ held.

....

ג [Heb: Gimel]

....

SLIDE # ?

Large blue Gimel against orange background.

....

HT:

Behold the Sacred Letter *Gimel*. With the light of Gimel, you sealed the
infinite Below. With the light of Gimel, the sphere of *the Moon* was created
in the Macrocosm. Gaze intently upon the letter *Gimel* and perhaps you will
hear the voice of the goddess Luna speak to your soul.

[Pause.]

HT: *[As Luna]*

I am Luna, the Moon. Goddess of the Lonely Wilderness, of Wild Animals,
and the Hunt. Why do you come to me?

WG: *[For Candidate, who repeats]*

It is my will to awaken to perfect realization of myself. I cannot awaken
to perfection until I have balanced within my soul the Blessings and the
Curses of Luna and Gimel.

HT: *[As Luna]*

You are wise and very brave to make such a fearsome request. It is true. When you awaken to my light, I freely pour my treasures upon you. A Rich Harvest of Delight is yours. I bring you *Peace*. Your dreams shall be pure and your visions clear and full of wisdom. These gifts are yours.

[Pause.]

....
SLIDE #?

Large orange Gimel against blue background.
....

But beware! My Light is so pure it is one with my Shadow, and my Shadow, when she stands, alone is a great sorceress. SHE will deceive you. She brings *War* and clouds your vision with illusions. She transforms your bright dreams to sterile, cold nightmares. She crumbles the *Foundation* of your sanity if you fall under her Spell. Do NOT look upon HER!

....
SLIDE #?

Total blackness.
....

[Pause.]

....
SLIDE # ?

Large blue Gimel against orange background.
....

WG:

Gaze deeply at the Sacred Letter *Gimel*. To the unawakened, it is the letter of *Peace and War*. Don't take your eyes from it.

....
SLIDE # ?

Slide changes to bright white; in doing so, creates the floating orange ghost image of Gimel in the Candidate's brain.
....

HT:

See now, with the eyes of your soul, the true color and image of Gimel. Close your eyes and implant it deep in the center of your brain.

[Pause.]

I now bless you. But be ever mindful that the Blessings of Luna and Gimel are a Curse; and the Curses of Luna and Gimel are a Blessing. You will know you have truly awakened when you see neither Curse nor Blessing.

....

SLIDE # ?

Total blackness.

....

MUSIC

Mid-range F# held.

....

ד [Heb: Daleth]

....

SLIDE # ?

Large green Daleth against red background.

....

HT:

Behold the Sacred Letter *Daleth*. With the light of Daleth, you sealed the infinite West. With the light of Daleth, the sphere of *Venus* was created in the Macrocosm. Gaze intently upon the letter *Daleth* and perhaps you will hear the voice of the goddess Venus speak to your soul.

[Pause.]

HT: *[As Venus]*

I am Venus. Goddess of Love, Sex, and Fertility. Why do you come to me?

WG: *[For Candidate, who repeats]*

It is my will to awaken to perfect realization of myself. I cannot awaken to perfection until I have balanced within my soul the Blessings and the Curses of Venus and Daleth.

HT: *[As Venus]*

You are wise and very brave to make such a fearsome request. It is true. When you awaken to my light, I freely pour my treasures upon you. A Rich Harvest of Delight is yours. Wisdom, Happiness, Love, Beauty, Kindness, Joy, and Art. These gifts are yours.

....

SLIDE # ?

Large red Daleth against green background.

....

But beware! My Light is so pure she is one with my Shadow, and my Shadow, when she stands alone, is a great sorceress. SHE will deceive you. She brings *Folly* and transforms Victory to defeat. She bleeds away all power to Love and be Loved. She drains you of your life force and leaves you a dead, empty shell if you fall under her Spell. Do NOT look upon HER!

....

SLIDE # ?

Total blackness.

....

[Pause.]

....

SLIDE # ?

Large green Daleth against red background.

....

WG:

Gaze deeply at the Sacred Letter *Daleth*. To the unawakened, it is the letter of *Wisdom and Folly*. Don't take your eyes from it.

....

SLIDE # ?

Slide changes to bright white; in doing so, creates the floating red ghost image of Daleth in the Candidate's brain.

....

HT:

See now, with the eyes of your soul, the true color and image of Daleth. Close your eyes and implant it deep in the center of your brain.

[Pause.]

I now bless you. But be ever mindful that the Blessings of Venus and Daleth are a Curse; and the Curses of Venus and Daleth are a Blessing. You will know you have truly awakened when you see neither Curse nor Blessing.

....

SLIDE # ?

Total blackness.

....

MUSIC

Mid-range B♭ held.

....

כ [Heb: Kaph]

....

SLIDE # ?

Large violet Kaph against yellow background.

....

HT:
Behold the Sacred Letter *Kaph*. With the light of Kaph, you sealed the infinite East. With the light of Kaph, the sphere of *Jupiter* was created in the Macrocosm. Gaze intently upon the letter *Kaph* and perhaps you will hear the voice of the god Jupiter speak to your soul.

[Pause.]

HT: *[As Jupiter]*
I am Jupiter, God of the Sky, and Lightning and Thunder, Giver of Gifts, and Protector of the State. Why do you come to me?

WG: *[For Candidate, who repeats]*
It is my will to awaken to perfect realization of myself. I cannot awaken to perfection until I have balanced within my soul the Blessings and the Curses of Jupiter and Kaph.

HT: *[As Jupiter]*
You are wise and very brave to make such a fearsome request. But if you awaken to my light, I freely pour my treasures upon you. A Rich Harvest of Delight is yours. *Wealth*, Popularity, Glory, Generosity, Fortune, Honors, Respect, and Great Authority. These gifts are yours.

....
SLIDE #?

Large yellow Kaph against violet background.
....

But beware! My light is so pure it is one with my Shadow, and my Shadow, when he stands alone, is a great sorcerer. He will deceive you. He brings *Poverty* and ruin upon you. Without *Mercy*, he smashes your honor and reputation and leaves you a miserly, friendless, and forgotten pauper. Do not fall under his Spell! Do NOT look upon HIM!

....
SLIDE # ?

Total blackness.
....

[Pause.]
....
SLIDE # ?

Large violet Kaph against yellow background.
....

WG:
Gaze deeply at the Sacred Letter *Kaph*. To the unawakened, it is the letter of *Wealth and Poverty*. Don't take your eyes from it.

....
SLIDE # ?

*Slide changes to bright white; in doing so, creates the floating
yellow ghost image of Kaph in the Candidate's brain.*
....

HT:

See now, with the eyes of your soul, the true color and image of Kaph. Close
your eyes and implant it deep in the center of your brain.

[Pause.]

I now bless you. But be ever mindful that the Blessings of Jupiter and Kaph
are a Curse; and the Curses of Jupiter and Kaph are a Blessing. You will
know you have truly awakened when you see neither Curse nor Blessing.

....
SLIDE # ?

Total blackness.
....

MUSIC

Mid-range C held.
....

פ [Heb: Peh]

....
SLIDE # ?

Large red Peh against green background.
....

HT:

Behold the Sacred Letter *Peh*. With the light of Peh, you sealed the infinite
North. With the light of Peh, the sphere of *Mars* was created in the
Macrocosm. Gaze intently upon the letter *Peh* and perhaps you will hear
the voice of the god Mars speak to your soul.

[Pause.]

HT: *[As Mars]*

I am Mars. God of War and Protector of the Crops. Why do you come to me?

WG: *[For Candidate, who repeats]*

It is my will to awaken to perfect realization of myself. I cannot awaken
to perfection until I have balanced within my soul the Blessings and the
Curses of Mars and Peh.

HT: *[As Mars]*

You are wise and very brave to make such a fearsome request. It is true. When you awaken to my light, I freely pour my treasures upon you. A Rich Harvest of Delight is yours. Beauty, Conquest and Strength in battle, Courage, Glory, and Dominion. These gifts are yours.

....

SLIDE # ?

Large green Peh against red background.

....

But beware! My Light is so pure he is one with my Shadow, and my Shadow, when he stands alone, is a great sorcerer. He will deceive you. He brings defeat to your battles. He takes from you your Power and Courage if you fall under his Spell. Do NOT look upon Him!

....

SLIDE # ?

Total blackness.

....

[Pause.]

....

SLIDE # ?

Large red Peh against green background.

....

WG:

Gaze deeply at the Sacred Letter *Peh*. To the unawakened, it is the letter of *Beauty and Ugliness*. Don't take your eyes from it.

....

SLIDE # ?

Slide changes to bright white; in doing so, creates the floating green ghost image of Peh in the Candidate's brain.

....

HT:

See now, with the eyes of your soul, the true color and image of Peh. Close your eyes and implant it deep in the center of your brain.

[Pause.]

I now bless you. But be ever mindful that the Blessings of Mars and Peh are a Curse; and the Curses of Mars and Peh are a Blessing. You will know you have truly awakened when you see neither Curse nor Blessing.

....

SLIDE # ?

Total blackness.

....

....

MUSIC

Mid-range D held.

....

ר [Heb: Resh]

....

SLIDE # ?

Large orange Resh against blue background.

....

HT:

Behold the Sacred Letter *Resh*. With the light of Resh, you sealed the infinite South. With the light of Resh, the sphere of Sol was created in the Macrocosm. Gaze intently upon the letter *Resh* and perhaps you will hear the voice of the god Sol speak to your soul.

[Pause.]

HT: *[As Sol]*

I am Sol, god of Music, Poetry, Prophesy, and Truth. Why do you come to me?

WG: *[For Candidate, who repeats]*

It is my will to awaken to perfect realization of myself. I cannot awaken to perfection until I have balanced within my soul the Blessings and the Curses of Sol and Resh.

HT: *[As Sol]*

You are wise and very brave to make such a fearsome request. It is true. When you awaken to my light, I freely pour my treasures upon you. A Rich Harvest of Delight is yours. *Fruitfulness*, Fame, Honor, Victory, Fairness, and Radiant Glory. These gifts are yours.

....

SLIDE # ?

Large blue Resh against orange background.

....

But beware! My Light is so pure he is one with my Shadow, and my Shadow, when he stands alone, is a great sorcerer. He will deceive you. He brings *Sterility*. He kills your Heart and drives you from the *Beauty* of the light into the dark bowels of the Earth; your name shall be forgotten forever if you fall under his Spell. Do NOT look upon HIM!

....

SLIDE # ?

Total blackness.

....

[Pause.]

....

SLIDE # ?

Large orange Resh against blue background.

....

WG:

Gaze deeply at the Sacred Letter *Resh*. To the unawakened, it is the letter of *Fruitfulness and Sterility*. Don't take your eyes from it.

....

SLIDE # ?

Slide changes to bright white; in doing so, creates the floating blue ghost image of Resh in the Candidate's brain.

....

HT:

See now, with the eyes of your soul, the true color and image of Resh. Close your eyes and implant it deep in the center of your brain.

[Pause.]

I now bless you. But be ever mindful that the Blessings of Sol and Resh are a Curse; and the Curses of Sol and Resh are a Blessing. You will know you have truly awakened when you see neither Curse nor Blessing.

....

SLIDE # ?

Total blackness.

....

MUSIC

Mid-range A held.

....

[Heb: Tav] ת

....

SLIDE # ?

Large black Hebrew Tav against white background.

....

HT:

Behold the Sacred Letter *Tav*, the Formless Primal Center.

Gaze intently upon the Letter *Tav* and perhaps you will hear the voice of the ancient god Saturn speak to your soul.

[Pause.]

HT: *[As Saturn]*
I am Saturn, God who made the gods. I am at once the Father and Mother of Existence itself. I am before and beyond Space and Time. I am the *Beginning* of All that *Was, Is,* and *Shall Be.* And I am the *End* of All that *Never Was, Never Is,* and *Never Shall Be . . . .* Tell me why you *think* you have come to me?

WG: *[For Candidate, who repeats]*
It is my will to awaken to perfect realization of myself. I cannot awaken to perfection until I have balanced within my soul the Blessings and the Curses of Saturn.

HT:
YOU ARE A FOOL to make such a fearsome request! Words and numbers and letters mean *nothing* to ME. In Me, no opposites exist. No Blessing. No Curse. In Me, all contradictions are reconciled. In Me, there is neither Good nor Evil. Death is one with Life, and the Darkness is one with the Light.

SLIDE # ?

Large white Hebrew Tav against black background.

To awaken to my mystery, you must slay the two-headed dragon of duality itself!

[Pause.]

SLIDE # ?

Large black Hebrew Tav against white background.

WG:
Gaze deeply at the Sacred Letter *Tav.* To the unawakened, it is the letter of *Dominion and Slavery.* Don't take your eyes from it.

SLIDE # ?

Slide changes to bright white; in doing so, creates the floating ghost image of Tav in the Candidate's brain.

[Pause.]

See now my true color with the eyes of your soul. Close your eyes and implant it deep in the center of your brain.

War and Peace, Life and Death, Wisdom and Folly, Fruitfulness and Sterility, Wealth and Poverty, Dominion and Slavery are not opposites . . . they are ONE! and NONE! within mine awakened Eye.

And *you*, my child, will awaken when you realize *your* eye and *mine eye* are the same *EYE*.

HT: *[Claps 3-1-3.]*
Let us now stand.

> *[WG removes cushions from the floorcloth. HT remains in the Center. WG and Candidate move to the west of the floorcloth.]*

IV

CLOSING CEREMONY

> *[Newly initiated Candidate stands in the west of the Temple and observes and follows directions.]*

HT: *[Claps 3-1-3.]*
Friends and Comrades, assist me to close this Second-Degree Temple of Our Holy Order. I direct our newly initiated Comrade to withdraw the Light once more into infinite darkness.

> *[WG helps Candidate extinguish the candles on the Menorah in the following order: orange, scarlet, violet, green, blue, yellow, black.]*

HT: *[Cont.]*
How peaceful and profound is this Darkness absolute. It swallows up even the thought of darkness and light.

> *[HT goes to the Altar of Light and relights the black Saturn candle in the center of the Menorah. The Temple is now lit only by this candle.]*

HT: *[Claps 3-1-3.]*
Worthy Guide, what is the hour?

WG:
Honored Teacher, it is the silent, dark moment before Light expands and shatters into vibrations of color and sound and shifting forms and pairs of opposites.

HT: *[Claps 3-1-3.]*
Worthy Guide, what is this place?

WG:
Light in Extension, Honored Teacher.

HT: *[Claps 3-1-3.]*
Worthy Guide, what is the source of *Light in Extension?*

WG:
Honored Teacher, it is hidden.

HT: *[Claps 3-1-3.]*
Worthy Guide, what God utters the Word that shatters the Light into vibrations of colors and sounds? What God speaks and seals the limits of Space and Form and Time?

WG:
The *Number Seven*, Honored Teacher—through the agency of the *Seven Double Letters* of the Hebrew alphabet. As it is written in the *Sepher Yezirah*:

> *There are seven, of which three are against three, and one places them in equilibrium.*[33]

The *Number Seven* seals the limits of Space and Form and Time; and by doing so divides itself *against* itself to become the God of opposing forces, qualities, and appearances—a God who sleeps and dreams it opposes a devil; a light that sleeps and dreams it opposes darkness.

HT:
But, Worthy Guide, is not this dream of the Number Seven the nature of all phenomena in the dimensional universe we perceive around us? Is it not the nature of objective reality?

WG:
Indeed, it is Honored Teacher, if we understand *reality* to be that which is perceived by those who are also trapped in the same dream.

- *Seven* is *phantom Life* that dreams of *Death.*

- *Seven* is *phantom Peace* that dreams of *War.*

- *Seven* is *phantom Wisdom* that dreams of *Folly.*

- *Seven* is *phantom Wealth* that dreams of *Poverty.*

- *Seven* is *phantom Beauty* that dreams of *Ugliness.*

- *Seven* is *phantom Fruitfulness* that dreams of *Sterility.*

- *Seven* is *phantom Dominion* that dreams of *Slavery.*

HT: *[Claps 3-1-3.]*
Worthy Guide, what do we call this world of duality?

WG:
Honored Teacher, it is called the *Macrocosm*, the "greater world" . . . for it casts a great spell—so great a spell the uninitiated believe the Macrocosm to be God, and the unawakened believe it to be Heaven.

HT:
What are the Seven Double Letters?

WG:
Beth and Gimel—Daleth and Kaph—Peh and Resh . . . and Tav.

HT:
And do these words have meaning?

WG:
Indeed, they do, Honored Teacher. Beth is a "House" and Gimel a "Camel"—Daleth a "Door" and Kaph the "Palm of a Hand"—Peh is the "Mouth" and Resh is the "Face" . . . and Tav is a "Cross" or a "Mark" that seals the gates of existence from within and without.

HT:
What are the duties of the Seven Double Letters?

WG:
- Beth and Gimel mount the Mother Letter *Aleph* and seal infinite Above and infinite Below.

- Daleth and Kaph mount the Mother Letter *Mem* and seal infinite East and infinite West.

- Peh and Resh mount the Mother Letter *Shin* and seal infinite North and infinite South.

HT:
And the Letter *Tav*? What position does Tav hold? What direction does Tav seal?

WG:
No position, Honored Teacher. No direction. Tav is the inscrutable source and center of the Macrocosm. From Tav burst the rays of the Three Mother Letters whose extension, in turn, creates Above/Below; East/West; North/South.

[HT faces WG. Both simultaneously give the Second-Degree Sign. They then exchange the Second-Degree Grip. They hold this gesture as they exchange the Second-Degree Word.]

HT:
MEN-

WG:
OR-

HT:
AH.

HT & WG: *[Together]*
MENORAH.

HT:
The Sign is made. The Grip is given. The Word is Spoken. I declare the Temple closed in the Second-Degree.

HT: *[Claps 3-1-3.]*

WG: *[Claps 3-1-3.]*

CANDIDATE: *[Claps 3-1-3.]*

ALL: *[Clap 3-1-3.]*

HT:
The Ceremony is ended.

V

PRESENTATION OF TOY
AND SECOND-DEGREE PORTFOLIO

[HT presents newly initiated Candidate with the Second-Degree Study Portfolio and Double-Letter Cube Toy.]

HT:
I once again take pleasure in presenting you with a sacred toy. You will use it often in the coming months in the study and exercise program we have assigned for you. It is the dimensional Cube of the Seven Double Letters. Above and Below are created by the yellow pipe cleaner of Aleph; East and West are created by the blue pipe cleaner of Mem; and North and South are

created by the red pipe cleaner of Shin. Hidden in the midst, at the primal center, is Tav.

When you understand the true meaning of this little toy, the DNA of your soul will be further mutated as it vibrates in harmony with the DNA of existence itself. *When you understand the true meaning of this little toy,* you will be *Master of the Seven Double Letters.*

Also, I present you with your Second-Degree Study Portfolio. Most importantly, it again contains a complete copy of the Initiation Ceremony you have just experienced. Study it well. Of all the materials appointed for your study, it is the most important because your initiation has further mutated you in a most fundamental and wonderful way. Memorize it like a song. Rehearse it daily in your memory and imagination. Relive the ceremony in your mind each night, as you compose yourself for sleep. By doing so, you will further rouse the soul's dreaming chrysalis to stir and awaken as the divine butterfly of Self.

The Seven Double Letters are now fertile seeds that have been implanted deep in your awakening soul. The seeds will continue to grow, but to assure their vitality, you must continue to nurture them with your persistent, loving attention. Do this, and you will surely awaken.

When you are Master of the Seven Double Letters, you will return to us and take the next step to your awakening.

O∴ H∴ O∴
SECOND-DEGREE
PORTFOLIO

FIGURE 10. SECOND-DEGREE MENORAH.

SECOND-DEGREE
STUDY PROGRAM

Nothing is too silly or frivolous if it provides the opportunity for you to familiarize yourself with the letters you are assigned to master.

Congratulations upon receiving your Second-Degree Initiation. We hope that the ceremony was for you both memorable and edifying, and that you feel generally enriched by the experience. The following material is intended to be suggestive of a course of study and practice to help you digest and process the mysteries and lessons of the Second-Degree and prepare you for the challenges that await you in the Third and final degree.

Hebrew Letter & English	Name #	Full Spelling #	Meaning	Planetary Sphere & Tarot Trump	Color	Flashing Color	Music Note	Qabalistic Intelligence	Position on Cube
ב B	Beth 2	ביח BITh 111	House	Mercury & Magician	Yellow	Violet	E	Intelligence of Transparency	Above
ג G	Gimel 3	גים MIM 90	Camel	Luna & High Priestess	Blue	Orange	G#	Uniting Intelligence	Below
ד D	Daleth 4	דלח DLTh 350	Door	Venus & Empress	Emerald Green	Red	F#	Illuminating Intelligence	East
כ K	Kaph 20 or 500 Final ך	כפ KP 100	Grasping Hand	Jupiter & Wheel of Fortune	Violet	Yellow	B♭	Intelligence of Conciliation	West
פ P F	Peh 80	פה PH 85	Mouth	Mars & Tower	Scarlet	Green	C	Active or Exciting Intelligence	North
ר R	Resh 200	ריש RISh 510	Face	Sun & Sun	Orange	Blue	D	Collecting Intelligence	South
ת Th T	Tav 400	תו TV 406	Mark, Cross	Saturn (& Element Earth) & Universe	Indigo	Deep Amber	A	Administrative Intelligence	Center

TABLE 2. TABLE OF THE SEVEN DOUBLE LETTERS.

PERPETUAL TINKERING

Please review what was said in your First-Degree Portfolio about the Table of Letters and perpetually tinkering with the letters. You will again need to refer to other books in your own Qabalah reference library, without which your Qabalistic calculations are impossible. For the Second-Degree, we especially recommend:

- *Sepher Yezirah*: Chapter IV

- *Chicken Qabalah*: Chapter III

And for other topics of general research:

- The Seven Planets of the Ancients (in Tree of Life order—Saturn, Jupiter, Mars, Sol, Venus, Mercury, Luna)

- Gods of Egyptian, Greek, and Roman mythology and their stories

- Colors of the rainbow and the musical octave

- Ideas of Duality and Opposites

In your journal, record your discoveries, revelations, or other Qabalistic synchronicities you observe.

INITIATION SCRIPT

It is your Great Work, as a Second-Degree Initiate, to deeply embed this ceremony in your psyche before proceeding to the Third-Degree.

Please review what was said in your First-Degree Portfolio.

SECOND-DEGREE TOY

Your Second-Degree toy is the simple cube presented to you at the conclusion of your initiation. It was created by your First-Degree toy when Aleph, Mem, and Shin extended to create dimensional space. Part of your assignment as a Second-Degree Initiate-Artist is to somehow properly unite the First-Degree toy with the Second-Degree toy so that it is obvious to the observer how one created the other.

You will *play* with this toy as a meditation aid when attuning yourself to the Three Mother Letters and the Seven Double Letters. You are encouraged to create your own larger and more substantial version on heavy paper or card stock. Color it with the appropriate colors and add whatever other appropriate correspondences you discover in your studies.

Have fun with your toy. Create Qabalistic games to play with it. Generate words, numbers, and divinatory oracles by ceremonially "rolling the dice." Nothing is too silly or frivolous if it provides the opportunity for you to familiarize yourself with the letters you are assigned to master. Keep a record of the results of such games.

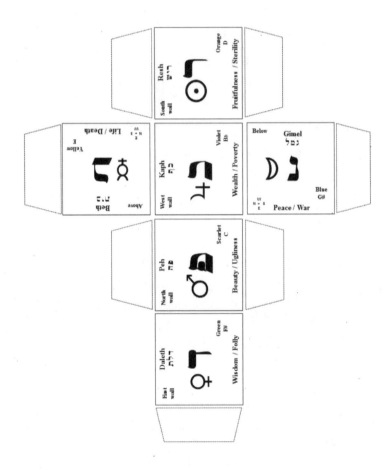

FIGURE 11. SECOND-DEGREE CUBE TOY.

SECOND-DEGREE ART ASSIGNMENT #1

Construct a Double-Letter Cube

Your first art assignment is relatively simple. When it is completed, you will be rewarded with a handsome example of your Second-Degree toy. You will need a little help from a copy machine, but that shouldn't be too hard to arrange.

1. Make a copy of Figure 11; you can even enlarge it a bit if you like. Print it on the heaviest white paper or card stock available to you.

2. Carefully cut out the pattern.

3. Fold at the appropriate lines and then fold into a simple box. Tape if necessary.

For a more advanced project, you may wish to paint the cube and the letters with the appropriate colors and flashing colors.

SECOND-DEGREE ART ASSIGNMENT #2

Flash Card Color Images of the Seven Double Letters

Your second art assignment is to create seven colored "flash cards" (one for each Double Letter) the same size and dimensions as the three you created for the Mother Letters. Do this by hand, not computer. You will find the appropriate colors itemized on the Table of the Seven Double Letters. For example, for Beth:

1. On a plain, *bright white* piece of 8½ × 11-inch heavy paper or card stock, lightly trace (in pencil) the outline of a large letter *Beth*.

2. Using *yellow* oil, acrylic, or watercolor paint or pens, carefully fill in the Beth. Be careful to cover over or otherwise erase the pencil line.

Make six more flash cards: one for Gimel (blue); one for Daleth (emerald green); one for Kaph (violet); one for Peh (scarlet); one for Resh (orange); and one for Tav (indigo-black).

Also, as before, have an extra plain, white sheet that will be used in the exercise.

And, as you are working on your art projects: Remember what was said in your First-Degree Portfolio about colors, fragrances, and sense associations while working with projects associated with the individual letters.

Your Second-Degree Home Temple

Now that you are a Second-Degree Initiate, you will wish to set up your own Second-Degree Temple arranged and decorated by objects, colors, sounds, textures, and fragrances associated with (or otherwise characterized by) the seven Double Letters, the seven Planetary Spheres, and art themes of *duality*.

Your Second-Degree Altar

Depending on what you used for your First-Degree Altar, you may not wish to radically change the basic shape or structure of your altar top. A common tabletop with a seven-sided figure or seven-pointed star design as the centerpiece would work admirably. Use your artist's imagination and sense of beauty.

Again, it will serve both as your *Altar of Incense* and your *Altar of Light*. You will replace the three-stemmed candelabra of the First-Degree with the seven-branched Menorah of the Second-Degree.

Setup Suggestions

Everything in your Second-Degree Temple should bring to your mind some quality or aspect of the number seven and the Seven Double Letters.

Your Temple should be illuminated by a seven-branched Menorah with colored candles (from left to right: red, green, yellow, black, blue, violet, and orange). Your Altar cloth and other hangings could reflect these same colors. Incense should be chosen to be suggestive of planetary influences. The seven Hebrew letters themselves should also be visible. Perhaps some Tarot art of the trumps: *Magician, High Priestess, Empress, Wheel of Fortune, Tower, Sun,* and *Universe.*

Once you start thinking about these things, the artist in you will get all sorts of ideas; you'll start seeing sevens *everywhere*. Soon your Second-Degree Temple will expand to become the entire world around you!

EXERCISES AND MEDITATIONS

These are a few exercises, meditations, and practices recommended for you as a Second-Degree Initiate. They are designed to attune you to the specific agencies and powers of consciousness associated with the Seven Double Letters of the Hebrew alphabet. Like those of the First-Degree, these exercises are not difficult and do not require a great deal of time to execute. It is hoped that you will continue with your daily routine and diligently follow it for a period of *ninety days*.

These exercises should be accompanied and enhanced (whenever possible and practical) by the appropriate incense or scents, music, and temple colors associated in your mind with the specific letter or letters being worked.

Once you have mastered these preliminary exercises, you are encouraged to design rituals and practices of your own based on your increasing mastery of the mysteries of the Seven Double Letters.

∴

SIMPLE SECOND-DEGREE HOME TEMPLE OPENING

[To be performed prior to other home rituals, exercises, or meditations.]

[Sit before the Altar. At the beginning, the candles of the Menorah are unlit.]

[Clap seven times 3-1-3.]

Darkness . . . before Light expands and shatters into colors, sounds, shifting forms, and pairs of opposites.

[Striking a match.]

Light in Extension.

[Lighting the center black Tav candle and plucking it from the Menorah.]

Seven seals the limits of Space and Form and Time; Seven divides itself *against* itself.

[Lighting the yellow Beth candle.]

Phantom *Life* that dreams of *Death*.

[Lighting the blue Gimel candle.]

Phantom *Peace* that dreams of *War*.

[Lighting the green Daleth candle.]

Phantom *Wisdom* that dreams of *Folly*.

[Lighting the violet Kaph candle.]

Phantom *Wealth* that dreams of *Poverty.*

[Lighting the red Peh candle.]

Phantom *Beauty* that dreams of *Ugliness.*

[Lighting the orange Resh candle.]

Phantom *Fruitfulness* that dreams of *Sterility.*

[Placing the lit black Tav candle back on the Menorah.]

Phantom *Dominion* that dreams of *Slavery.*

Three are against three, and one places them in equilibrium.

The Temple is Illuminated.

[Clap seven times 3-1-3.]

The Temple is open.

∴

AMSH WARM-UP EXERCISE
[Exercise from First-Degree is still recommended.]

∴

DAWN AMSH BREATH CYCLE
[Exercise from First-Degree is still recommended.]

∴

PASSING THE PYLONS
Astral Projection into the
World of the Double Letters

The purpose of the exercise is to attune and acclimate your psychic body to the particular frequency of consciousness (Qabalistic Intelligence) exemplified by each Double Letter (see description in Second-Degree Portfolio) by projecting one's consciousness through the color-polarized floating "ghost image" of the letter, by means of the technique employed in the initiation ceremonies.

Materials Needed:

- Pitch pipe

- Flash cards of Seven Double Letters

    ◦ Yellow *Beth*

    ◦ Blue *Gimel*

    ◦ Emerald green *Daleth*

    ◦ Violet *Kaph*

    ◦ Scarlet *Peh*

    ◦ Orange *Resh*

    ◦ Black *Tav*

- Blank white card

- Bright light

∴

PASSING THE PYLONS
Skrying Exercise

[Review First-Degree Portfolio.]

Example: Beth

1. Carefully mount your blank white flash card at the *center right* of your Altar; and directly beside it (at the *center left* of the Altar), mount your yellow Beth flash card.

2. Shine a bright light in such a way that it vibrantly illuminates both cards but does not shine into your eyes.

3. Comfortably seat yourself as near as possible to the two cards so that when you gaze at the letter, it essentially fills your field of vision.

4. Take your pitch pipe, find the E note, and blow.

5. Take a deep breath and forcefully sing, "Bahhhhhhh." *(Repeat three times.)*

6. Relax and gaze at the brightly illuminated yellow Beth. Keep staring at the letter until it starts to do strange things.

7. Then quickly turn your gaze to the plain white blank card.

   a. You should see a *violet* Beth floating over the white card. That ghost image is your gateway—your pylon.

   b. If you close your eyes and wait for a moment, the violet ghost Beth will clearly appear on the screen of your inner eyelids and remain floating for several seconds. If this doesn't happen, repeat steps 6 and 7 until it does.

8. When you have mastered the art of creating the ghost image of the letter on the screen of your closed eyes, you'll be ready to project your consciousness through the pylon and enter in vision the "world" of the letter.

9. The moment the ghost image is firmly visible on your closed eyes, make the First-Degree Sign[1] and whisper "Ahhhhhhh-Mmmmmmmm-Shhhhhhh" and imagine yourself passing through the violet letter *Beth* as if it were a letter-shaped puff of smoke.

10. Now, just relax and begin your skrying session.

11. When you sense you have "seen" enough for this session, use your imagination to pass back into your Temple by again giving the First-Degree Sign and Word. Then open your eyes and clap three times.

12. Important: Review notes on skrying from your First-Degree Portfolio. Immediately write down in your journal the details of *everything* you saw or everything you thought about during the skrying session. Don't omit anything, no matter how insignificant you might think it is. Try to "bring back" a symbol from your vision. You will analyze it later.

Beth

Image on card:	Yellow Beth
Pitch pipe note:	E
Word sung:	Bahhhhhhh
Ghost Beth:	Violet

The procedure for the six other Double Letters (Gimel, Daleth, Kaph, Peh, Resh, and Tav) is exactly as in the Beth example, but with appropriate changes to colors, musical notes, and words vibrated.

Gimel

Image on card:	Blue Gimel
Pitch pipe note:	G$^{\#}$
Word sung:	Gahhhhhhh
Ghost Gimel:	Orange

Kaph

Image on card:	Violet Kaph
Pitch pipe note:	B$^{\flat}$
Word sung:	Kahhhhhhh
Ghost Kaph:	Yellow

Resh

Image on card:	Orange Resh
Pitch pipe note:	D
Word sung:	Rahhhhhhh
Ghost Resh:	Blue

Daleth

Image on card:	Emerald green Daleth
Pitch pipe note:	F$^{\#}$
Word sung:	Dahhhhhh
Ghost Daleth:	Red

Peh

Image on card:	Scarlet Peh
Pitch pipe note:	C
Word sung:	Pahhhhhh
Ghost Peh:	Green

Tav

Image on card:	Indigo Tav
Pitch pipe note:	A
Word sung:	Thahhhhhh
Ghost Tav:	Deep Amber

THIRD-DEGREE

Preliminary Notes

This version of the script is written assuming the Candidate is female.[1] Individuals wishing to perform or exemplify this ritual are encouraged to make all changes necessary to accommodate any gender identification.

It is preferred (though not absolutely necessary) that the Third-Degree Initiation be conferred in its entirety for one Candidate at a time. Ideally, the ceremony is scheduled no sooner than three months (ninety days) following the Second-Degree Initiation. It is a rather lengthy ceremony. As in the First-Degree, there is a long break for a celebratory banquet and rest period, after which all return late in the evening for a final meditation.

The Candidate must verbally affirm his or her familiarity with the Second-Degree Study Material, but no formal examination or proficiency test is administered.

IMPORTANT NOTE ON SAFETY:

O∴ H∴ O∴ initiations should never (at any time before, during, or after the ceremony) be the occasion to frighten, belittle, or humiliate the Candidate, who at all times shall be treated with the utmost courtesy and respect.

SPECIAL THIRD-DEGREE SAFETY NOTE:

An essential aspect of the Third-Degree Initiation experience is that the Candidate undergo a series of slight but memorable moments of harmless physical discomfort so that he or she will permanently associate the "trauma" with lessons of each of the twelve letters that are the subject of the Degree. Specifically, twelve times during the course of the Third-Degree ceremony, the Candidate is presented a long-stemmed rose (*untrimmed* of thorns) to hold for a length of time. It is intended that the thorns present an irritating impediment to the candidate's painless handling of the rose. It is likely (and, in fact, intended) that the candidate accidentally prick his or her fingers or hands at some point in the process.

Therefore, to prevent any possibility of infection, each rose stem and thorn must be carefully cleaned and sterilized prior to the ceremony. After the ceremony, the candidate shall be required to thoroughly wash any breaks in the skin and, if necessary, scratches shall be treated with antibacterial cream and covered with a clean bandage before proceeding with the ceremony.[2]

PRELUDE TO THE THIRD-DEGREE INITIATION CEREMONY

Officer's Script

[The officers are the same as in the First-Degree and Second-Degree ceremonies, and the Temple is at first arranged exactly as for a First-Degree Initiation except that the Altar of Light now supports both the three-branch candelabra of the First-Degree and the seven-branch Menorah of the Second-Degree.]

[The Temple is ceremonially opened in the First-Degree,[3] then immediately opened in the Second-Degree.[4] (First and Second-Degree floorcloths are not employed in these openings.)]

[The Candidate for the Third-Degree Initiation is present in the Temple during the First- and Second-Degree Openings.]

[Candidate stands in the center of the Temple west of HT's chair.]

[At the conclusion of the First-Degree Opening, the Temple is illuminated only by the three candles of the candelabra.]

[The First-Degree Opening concludes when HT says . . .]

HT: *[Claps three times.]*
The Sign is made. The Grip is given. The Word is Spoken. I declare the Temple open in the First-Degree.

[Officers immediately proceed to open in the Second-Degree.[5] At the conclusion of Second-Degree Opening, the Temple is still illuminated only by the three candles of the candelabra and by the single Tav candle of the Menorah.]

[The Second-Degree Opening concludes when HT says . . .]

HT: *[Claps 3-1-3.]*
The Sign is made. The Grip is given. The Word is Spoken. I declare the Temple open in the Second-Degree.

[HT is seated. Candidate and WG remain standing.]

HT: *[Claps 444-444-444.]*
Worthy Guide, assist me now to open the *Temple of the Twelve Letters.* Satisfy yourself that all present are *Masters of the Twelve Letters.*

WG: *[Turns and loudly addresses the Candidate.]*
Let all present stand to order and present themselves as *Masters of the Twelve Letters.* All give the *Sign* of the Third-Degree.

[There is a pause while the Candidate, obviously confused and unable to give the Sign, fails to comply.]

WG: *[Turns and addresses HT.]*
Honored Teacher, I have discovered there is a *Master of the Three and Seven Letters* present among us, but she has failed to demonstrate the proper Tokens that would prove her to be Master of the Twelve Letters. She does not bear the *twelve scars of battle*, nor has she risen, by wisdom, above the dream of perpetual war.

HT:
Worthy Guide, do not be quick to condemn our Sister's intrusion upon our mysteries. Let us not forget that time and again she has demonstrated the purity of her aspiration to awaken from her dreams. *(addressing Candidate)* Friend and Comrade, once more you find yourself in the awkward position of intruding uninvited where you are not presently qualified to be. As Master of the Three and Seven Letters, you are armed with only a portion of the sacred alphabet of creation. *Twelve Simple Letters* remain for you to master before you are fluent in the language of God. However illiterate and inarticulate you may presently be, I must ask you to search your heart for words that might explain to us why you have come to us today, and why you are resolved to present yourself for Third-Degree Initiation?

[The Candidate is encouraged to briefly explain her desire to advance to the Third-Degree, and if necessary, HT holds an impromptu and informal discussion with her. HT and WG should make mental note of key issues in Candidate's stated desires, and, if the opportunity later presents itself, address those personal issues specifically during the evening Banquet.]

[Done.]

HT:
Your words ring true and reveal to us you are indeed in the process of awakening. This pleases us, for in fact . . . *we need you.* Indeed, without *you*, none of us would be here—none of this would be happening. Recall my words from your First-Degree Initiation:

> *In truth, you are the only member of Our Holy Order.*
> *You are the Honored Teacher. You are the Worthy Guide.*
> *You are the temple, and you are the teachings. You are the*
> *shrine, and you are the God within the shrine.*

For the moment, however, this reality remains for you purely theoretical. So, for the moment, let us simply say that you have reached the level in Our Holy Order where you must come to the full realization that you are no longer merely the Candidate, but are, in fact, the *key officer* of your own initiation. And so, I ask you to linger with us a moment longer and assist us in our work—for **three** Masters of the Three and Seven Letters are required to properly Illuminate the Third-Degree Temple before work can begin.

> *[At this point the Temple is still lighted only by the three candles*
> *of the candelabra and by the single Tav candle of the Menorah.]*

> *[WG goes to the Altar of Incense and adds*
> *more incense to the charcoal.]*

> *[HT rises from his chair and walks to the*
> *area just east of the Altar of Light.]*

HT:
Worthy Guide, please escort our Sister to west of the Altar of Light.

> *[Done. WG stands to Candidate's right to assist.]*

HT: *[Cont.]*
We meet at the Altar of Light to enlist your assistance to illuminate the Temple; for the Sacred Light comes not from the glow of lamps and candles, or even from the fire of the Sun or from the stars. The Sacred Light comes from *you*, and you alone. Dear Sister, are you prepared to claim your birthright as the Sacred Light?

CANDIDATE:
Yes.

HT: *[Cont.]*
Then I say to you: Seek yourself first in the Darkness; for in truth, if you cannot discover the Light in the *Darkness*, you will never discover it

anywhere. Please extinguish these dream flames with the spirit of your living breath.

> *[Candidate blows out the candles, plunging*
> *the Temple into absolute darkness.*
>
> *All maintain silence for approximately thirty seconds.]*

HT:
How peaceful and profound is this Darkness Divine. Such is God-consciousness. No name. No form. No nature. No dream of light. No dream of time. No dream of space. No dream of motion. No dream . . . not even the dream of Self. Nothing to cleave the sweet Darkness and deface this absolute, infinite, and eternal bliss.

> *[HT lights a long-burning match.]*[6]

HT: *[Cont.]*
But Absolute Self yearned to know itself—to identify itself. It hungered for Self-Awareness. So, in order to touch itself—in order to experience its own infinite nature, it forsook the paradise of Selfless Self and entered a master-dream of all possible possibilities. It concentrated its Absoluteness into a seed of infinite *potentiality*—a Formless Primal Nothingness, *from which* ALL that *can ever be* proceeds; and a Nothingness *into which* ALL that could *ever be* returns.

> *[HT lights the black Tav candle of the Menorah.]*

HT: *[Cont.]*
The Absolute sealed its *self* into itself as the Sacred Letter *Tav*. The signature of God.

> *[WG plucks the lighted black Tav candle from the*
> *Menorah and presents it to the Candidate. For the*
> *moment, it is the only light in the Temple.]*

HT: *[Cont.]*
Tav said, "I AM," and collapsed its Nothingness into a dream *Point—a Singularity* without size or position; for indeed, there was no place for the Point to dwell but inside itself.

> *[WG quietly instructs the Candidate to use*
> *the flame of the black Tav candle to light the*
> *yellow Aleph candle on the candelabra.]*

HT: *[Cont.]*
And with the Light of the Mother Letter *Aleph*, the Point created a line that extended upwards and downwards, creating the infinitely ascending *Above* and the infinitely descending *Below*.

[WG quietly instructs the Candidate to use the flame of the black Tav candle to light the blue Mem candle on the candelabra.]

HT: *[Cont.]*
And with the Light of the Mother Letter *Mem*, the Point created a second line that extended to the *right* and to the *left*, creating the infinitely extending *East* and *West*.

[WG quietly instructs the Candidate to use the flame of the black Tav candle to light the red Shin candle on the candelabra.]

HT: *[Cont.]*
And with the Light of the Mother Letter *Shin*, the Point created a third line that extended directly in *front* and directly in *back* of itself, creating the infinitely extending *North* and *South*.

[WG quietly instructs the Candidate to replace the black Tav candle to its place on the Menorah. For the moment, it and the three candles of the candelabra are the only lights in the Temple.]

HT: *[Cont.]*
Thus was the dream-consciousness of Space itself created. And the dream of movement within Space creates *Time*.

[WG instructs the Candidate to pluck the lighted yellow Aleph candle from the candelabra.]

HT: *[Cont.]*
Swirling like planets within this new and deeper dream of expanding Space-Time, the *Seven Double Letters* formed—seven dualities of the progressively fragmenting consciousness of God.

The extending line of *Aleph* created *Beth* (to seal the *Above*) and *Gimel* (to seal the *Below*), and in doing so created the Planetary Spheres of *Mercury* and *Luna*.

[WG quietly instructs the Candidate to use the flame of the yellow Aleph candle to light the yellow Beth and the blue Gimel candles on the Menorah.]

*[WG quietly instructs the Candidate to replace
the lighted yellow Aleph candle on the candelabra
and pluck the blue Mem candle.]*

HT: *[Cont.]*

The extending line of *Mem* created *Daleth* to seal the *East,* and *Kaph* to seal the *West*, and in doing so created the Planetary Spheres of *Venus* and *Jupiter*.

*[WG quietly instructs the Candidate to use the flame
of the blue Mem candle to light the green Daleth
and the violet Kaph candles on the Menorah.]*

*[WG quietly instructs the Candidate to replace the lighted blue
Mem candle on the candelabra and pluck the red Shin candle.]*

HT: *[Cont.]*

The extending line of *Shin* created *Peh* to seal the *North*, and *Resh* to seal the *South,* and in doing so created the Planetary Spheres of *Mars* and *Sol*.

*[WG quietly instructs the Candidate to use the
flame of the red Shin candle to light the scarlet Peh
and the orange Resh candles on the Menorah.]*

*[WG quietly instructs the Candidate to replace the
lighted red Shin candle on the candelabra.]*

HT:

Behold! The Temple Illuminated by the Three and Seven Letters!

WG:

But Honored Teacher, what of the first flame? The one from which all other lights were kindled. What of the *Double Letter Tav*, the Formless Primal Center? Is not Tav one of the Seven? Is not Tav a Planetary Sphere?

HT:

Yes, Worthy Guide. Tav is the Sphere of *Saturn*, but Saturn is unique among Planetary Spheres. On the *Tree of Life*, Saturn is the third sacred Emanation of the Supernal Triad that dwells above the terrible Abyss that separates pure God-consciousness from the fragments of dreams we mistake for reality. Saturn is older than the Gods and dwells in a palace quite above, within, and beyond the six spheres of the Macrocosm. . . .

WG: *[As if interrupting HT in mid-sentence]*

Honored Teacher, let us remember that our Comrade is as yet ill-armed to approach that mystery. Her quiver still lacks twelve arrows. She has not yet been blooded in the *War of Roses*.

HT: *[As if catching himself]*
Worthy Guide, you are correct. Let us proceed. I direct you to escort our Comrade to a place of solitude and quiet reflection.

[Addressing the Candidate]

Comrade, I recommend that during your meditations you will search deep in your heart to identify those aspects of your inner and outer life that are for you a source of perpetual *conflict*. Write them in your journal to memorialize this moment of reflection.

Do not do this as a confession, nor an exercise in self-incrimination. We simply ask that you use your time of reflection to identify and acknowledge the disruptive battles that rage unresolved within your soul.

*[WG escorts the Candidate out of the
Temple to the waiting area.]*[7]

*[WG returns to the Temple and assists HT in rearranging the
room for the Third-Degree Opening and Initiation Ceremony.]*

O∴ H∴ O∴
OUR HOLY ORDER
CEREMONY OF INITIATION
THIRD-DEGREE
Officer's Script

FIGURE 12.

OFFICERS

(Officers are the same as in the Ceremony
of the First- and Second-Degrees.)

(For the Third-Degree, HT and WG wear their hoods up.)

Sign, Grip, and Word of the Third-Degree

The Third-Degree *Sign* is given as follows:

- Raise both hands in front of face, palms flat, facing each other, fingers pointing upwards, thumbs pointing at eyes.

- Clap hands once.

- Then give "thumbs-up" gesture with both hands (still at eye level).

The Third-Degree *Grip* (includes the exchange of the **Word**) is given as follows:

- First person raises right hand, palm forward (as if to invite a "high-five" congratulatory hand slap), and says, "Balance."

- Second person does the same and says, "Harmony."

- Both slap hands and say together, "Beauty."

- First person smiles and gives thumbs-up gesture with right hand.

- Second person smiles and gives thumbs-up gesture with right hand.

Miscellaneous items to have on hand for the ceremony:

- For the Candidate:
  o Black hooded robe
  o Third-Degree cube toy (same as Second-Degree toy but with the Twelve Simple Letters added to the edges. This cube toy remains in the waiting area.)
  o Dodecahedron toy
  o Twelve stemmed red roses with thorns (to be arranged on floorcloth)
  o Light ceremonial sword
  o Third-Degree Study Portfolio

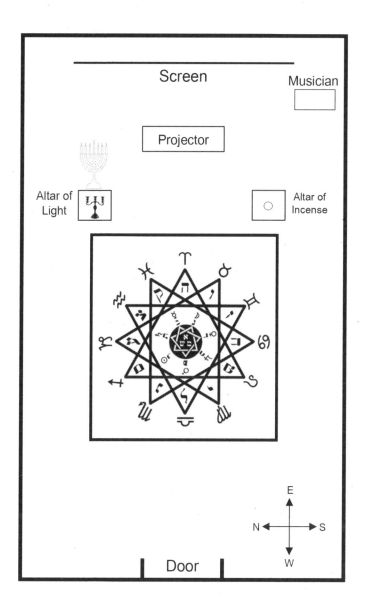

FIGURE 13. THIRD-DEGREE TEMPLE WITH FLOORCLOTH.

- There are no chairs for the Third-Degree Temple. As in the Second-Degree ceremony, three cushions for the fourth section are concealed until needed. Until then, officers and Candidate stand throughout.

- As in the First- and Second-Degree Temples, a large projection screen is set up in the East, and a *projector* rests on a small table in front of the screen at an appropriate distance to project images on the screen.

- The *Musician's station* remains concealed south of the screen: (*Musician*, being concealed, may, of course, remain seated.) As in the previous degrees, musical and tonal cues will again be played during certain sections of the ceremony. The organ (or electronic device) and the remote-control device for the projector are concealed in a place convenient for Musician to operate.

- The *Altar of Incense*, upon which rests a censer of smoking frankincense or other sweet-smelling resinous wood gum, remains in the South. (The *Altar of Incense* may need to be moved slightly from its precise Second-Degree position to accommodate the Third-Degree *floorcloth*.)

- A light ceremonial sword (which will be presented to the Candidate) is placed on the Altar of Incense.

- *The Altar of Light* remains in the North. (The *Altar of Light* may also need to be moved slightly from its precise Second-Degree position to accommodate the Third-Degree *floorcloth*.)

- The three-candle *candelabra* (which was used in the First-Degree) is returned to the Altar of Light and placed a few inches in front of the *Second-Degree "Menorah."* Candelabra and Menorah are fully charged with fresh colored candles arranged appropriately.

  Note: If all transpires correctly during the Ceremony of Illumination, all ten candles should already be burning at the beginning of the Third-Degree Opening.

- The Third-Degree Dodecahedron (described in the Third-Degree Portfolio) is also placed on the Altar of Light.

- Twelve Red Roses: Before the Candidate is brought in for initiation, one red rose (stemmed, with many thorns) is laid inside each of the twelve zodiac "points" of the floorcloth star. During the course of the ceremony, the Candidate will be required to pick up and hold all twelve roses (some minor discomfort is intended).

NOTES CONCERNING THE FLOORCLOTH:

The *floorcloth* again plays a very important role in the Third-Degree Initiation.[1] It is a square carpet (approximately 7 by 7 feet) made of canvas, oilcloth, linen, or any convenient cloth material of substantial thickness; and painted with the twelve-pointed star with Hebrew letters and astrological symbols arranged as shown in Figure 14. The background of the floorcloth is white or a light, neutral tone.

FIGURE 14. THIRD-DEGREE FLOORCLOTH.

I

OPENING CEREMONY

*[The Opening ceremony is performed by the Honored
Teacher (HT) and Worthy Guide (WG).]*

*[WG returns to the Temple and assists HT in rearranging
the room for the Third-Degree. They unroll and position
the Third-Degree floorcloth as illustrated. They place
one red rose (with a medium-length stem still bearing
all its thorns) near each of the twelve signs of the
zodiac at the twelve points of the floorcloth's star.]*

*[When all is ready, HT stands in the East just
beyond the Aries point of the floorcloth.]*

HT: *[Claps 4-4-4.]*
Worthy Guide, assist me to open the Temple in the Third-Degree.

*[WG joins HT in the East, where they exchange the
Sign, Grip, and Word of the Third-Degree.]*

HT:
The Sign is made. The Grip is given. The Word is Spoken. I declare the
Temple open in the Third-Degree.

HT: *[Claps 4-4-4.]*

WG: *[Claps 4-4-4.]*

HT:
Worthy Guide, bring the Candidate-in-waiting to the threshold of the
Temple door.

II

THE WAR OF ROSES

*[WG goes to the waiting area and collects the Candidate
and leads her to the Temple door. It is open. They are met
by HT, who stands just inside the threshold holding a light
ceremonial sword, his countenance stern and serious.]*

HT:
Comrade, arm yourself and join us.

> *[HT reaches across the threshold and hands Candidate
> the sword (blade pointed downward). WG hurriedly
> ushers the somewhat-confused Candidate inside
> the Temple and closes the door behind them.]*

HT: *[Cont.]*
The *War of Roses* is about to begin. Blood may be shed. Come!

> *[HT moves to east of the floorcloth. WG guides
> Candidate to the center of the floorcloth and stands
> behind and to just to the right of the Candidate.]*

HT: *[Claps 4-4-4.]*
Worthy Guide, what is the hour?

WG:
Honored Teacher, it is the hour of war.

HT: *[Claps 4-4-4.]*
Who are the combatants in this war?

WG:
The *Twelve Simple Letters* of the Sacred Hebrew alphabet: *Heh, Vav, Zain,
Cheth, Teth, Yod, Lamed, Nun, Samekh, Ayin, Tzaddi,* and *Qoph.* They war
within themselves and among each other—for *conflict* is their nature at this
level of dream consciousness.

HT: *[Claps 4-4-4.]*
Worthy Guide, why do they do battle?

WG:
Honored Teacher, as in all wars, there is ultimately no *reasonable* motive
for conflict. The combatants have forgotten themselves and fallen so

deeply asleep, they have poisoned the cast of characters that populate their dreams. They self-identify only as pieces of pieces of pieces of the *One-and-indivisible*. They war like tormented children, blindly discharging the elemental and planetary fragments that blindly animate them. In their fevered dreams of separation, they fight never-ending battles to plant flags of vain victory atop phantom hilltops.

HT:
Worthy Guide, what is the battlefield?

WG:
Honored Teacher, it is the twelve edges of the expanding Cube. It is reflected in the Heavens as the belt of the zodiac. It is the field of battle where the myriad forces of elements, planets, powers, and principles all attract and repel each other and form perpetually shifting alliances, hostilities, truces, marriages, and betrayals.

[WG picks up the Dodecahedron.]

[WG guides the Candidate to the Heh/Aries point of the star.]

 [Heb: Heh]

WG: *[Loudly shaking the Dodecahedron]*
All substance lives and struggles evermore

Through countless shapes continually at war,

By countless interactions interknit:[2]

HT:
Behold the letter *Heh!* To one who is awakened, *Heh* is the monogram of pure God-consciousness. But for those who linger yet in dream, *Heh* is a "Window" and alludes to the sense of "Sight." Your eye is a *window* out of which you peer to see the outside world, and a *window* into which the world peers to view the secrets of your soul.

In the dream of space-time, *Heh* is the zodiac sign *Aries*, cardinal sign of Fire—Aries, who is ruled by strong, active, and warlike Mars—Aries, where the virile and self-assured Sun, source of all manifest life around us, is lifted up and grows strong and rejoicing when he passes through the Sign of Aries.

The *countless interactions interknit* between Heh/Aries and all the other letters (whose elements, planets, and signs stand in harmony *with* or hostility *to* Fire, Mars, and the Sun) chart the ever-changing battle plans of the dream-wars of Heh.

Seize now the Rose of Heh and press its thorny stem against the upper blade of your sword so the beauty of the flower crowns and adorns the cross-guard of the hilt.

[WG assists Candidate if necessary.]

[Done.]

HT: *[Cont.]*
The dream of pain, the dream of pleasure. The battles of the letter *Heh* are never resolved while we dream . . . but only when we awaken.

[WG guides the Candidate to the Vav/Taurus point of the star.]

ו [Heb: Vav]

WG: *[Loudly shaking the Dodecahedron]*
All substance lives and struggles evermore

Through countless shapes continually at war,

By countless interactions interknit:

HT:
Behold the letter *Vav*! To one who is awakened, *Vav* is the monogram of pure God-consciousness. But for those who linger yet in dream, *Vav* is a "Nail" and alludes to the sense of "Hearing." As a nail penetrates two objects to bind them together, Vav joins darkness to light, man to woman, God to humanity. Vav is the nail that crucifies you to both your vices and your virtues, to your healthy habits or your unhealthy habits.

In the dream of space-time, *Vav* is the zodiac sign *Taurus*, the fixed Sign of Earth—Taurus who is ruled by beautiful, self-indulgent, and peaceful-loving Venus—Taurus where the Moon is lifted up and grows strong and rejoicing when she passes through the Sign of Taurus.

The *countless interactions interknit* between Vav/Taurus and all the other letters (whose elements, planets, and signs stand in harmony *with* or hostility *to* Earth, Venus, and the Moon) chart the ever-changing battle plans of the dream-wars of Vav.

Seize now the Rose of Vav and press its thorny stem against the upper blade of your sword so the beauty of the flower crowns and adorns the cross-guard of the hilt.

[WG assists Candidate if necessary.]

[Done.]

HT: *[Cont.]*
The dream of pain; the dream of pleasure. The battles of the letter *Vav* are never resolved while we dream . . . but only when we awaken.

> *[WG guides the Candidate to the Zain/Gemini point of the star.]*

[Heb: Zain]

WG: *[Loudly shaking the Dodecahedron]*
All substance lives and struggles evermore

Through countless shapes continually at war,

By countless interactions interknit:

HT:
Behold the letter *Zain*! To one who is awakened, *Zain* is the monogram of pure God-consciousness. But for those who linger yet in dream, *Zain* is a "Sword" and alludes to the discerning sense of "Smell." As sword cleaves a head from a body, Zain distinguishes wisdom from foolishness, truth from falsehood. Zain is the sword that can separate you from dangerous or unworthy influences or isolate you from enlightenment.

In the dream of space-time, *Zain* is the zodiac sign *Gemini*, the Mutable Sign of Air—Gemini who is ruled by playful, communicative, and slyly deceptive Mercury.

The *countless interactions interknit* between Zain/Gemini and all the other letters (whose elements, planets, and signs stand in harmony *with* or hostility *to* Air and Mercury) chart the ever-changing battle plans of the dream-wars of Zain.

Seize now the Rose of Zain and press its thorny stem against the upper blade of your sword so the beauty of the flower crowns and adorns the cross-guard of the hilt.

> *[WG assists Candidate if necessary.]*

> *[Done.]*

HT: *[Cont.]*
The dream of pain; the dream of pleasure. The battles of the letter *Zain* are never resolved while we dream . . . but only when we awaken.

> *[WG guides the Candidate to the Cheth/*
> *Cancer point of the star.]*

[Heb: Cheth]

WG: *[Loudly shaking the Dodecahedron]*
All substance lives and struggles evermore

Through countless shapes continually at war,

By countless interactions interknit:

HT:
Behold the letter *Cheth*! To one who is awakened, *Cheth* is the monogram of pure God-consciousness. But for those who linger yet in dream, *Cheth* is a "Fence" and alludes to the faculty of "Speech." Like a suit of armor, the fence isolates and protects the life within from outside influences. *Cheth* is a crust, a shell, and a membrane; *Cheth* is the Holy Grail that enfolds each monad of living existence.

In the dream of space-time, *Cheth* is the zodiac sign *Cancer*, the Cardinal Sign of Water—Cancer, who is ruled by the sensitive, reflective, and ever-changing Moon. Cancer, where benevolent, expansive, and philosophical Jupiter is lifted up and grows strong and rejoicing when he passes through the Sign of Cancer.

The *countless interactions interknit* between Cheth/Cancer and all the other letters (whose elements, planets, and signs stand in harmony *with* or hostility *to* Water, the Moon, and Jupiter) chart the ever-changing battle plans of the dream-wars of Cheth.

Seize now the Rose of Cheth and press its thorny stem against the upper blade of your sword so the beauty of the flower crowns and adorns the cross-guard of the hilt.

[WG assists Candidate if necessary.]

[Done.]

HT: *[Cont.]*
The dream of pain; the dream of pleasure. The battles of the letter *Cheth* are never resolved while we dream . . . but only when we awaken.

[WG guides the Candidate to the Teth/Leo point of the star.]

 [Heb: Teth]

WG: *[Loudly shaking the Dodecahedron]*
All substance lives and struggles evermore

Through countless shapes continually at war,

By countless interactions interknit:

HT:
Behold the letter *Teth*! To one who is awakened, *Teth* is the monogram of pure God-consciousness. But for those who linger yet in dream, *Teth* is a "Serpent" and alludes to the process of "Swallowing and Digestion." Long the symbol of wisdom, the image of the Serpent triggers within us an instinctual recollection of the fire of sexual ecstasy and the secret energy that courses up and down our spine.

In the dream of space-time, *Teth* is the zodiac sign *Leo*, the Fixed Sign of Fire—Leo, who is ruled by the virile and self-assured Sun, source of all manifest life around us.

The *countless interactions interknit* between Teth/Leo and all the other letters (whose elements, planets, and signs stand in harmony *with* or hostility *to* Fire and the Sun) chart the ever-changing battle plans of the dream-wars of Teth.

Seize now the Rose of Teth and press its thorny stem against the upper blade of your sword so the beauty of the flower crowns and adorns the cross-guard of the hilt.

[WG assists Candidate if necessary.]

[Done.]

HT: *[Cont.]*
The dream of pain; the dream of pleasure. The battles of the letter *Teth* are never resolved while we dream . . . but only when we awaken.

[WG guides the Candidate to the Yod/Virgo point of the star.]

[Heb: Yod]

WG: *[Loudly shaking the Dodecahedron]*
All substance lives and struggles evermore

Through countless shapes continually at war,

By countless interactions interknit:

HT:

Behold the letter *Yod*! To one who is awakened, *Yod* is the monogram of pure God-consciousness. But for those who linger yet in dream, *Yod* is a "Hand" and alludes to the sense of "Touch." The human hand, with its four finger-servants of a master opposable thumb, was the creative member with which humans first conquered fire, then the tools to conquer the world around us; *Yod* is the small creative source-flame, whose flickering creates the other letters of our sacred alphabet.

In the dream of space-time, *Yod* is the zodiac sign *Virgo*, the Mutable Sign of Earth—Virgo, who is ruled by playful, communicative, and slyly deceptive Mercury. Virgo, where mischievous and restless Mercury is also lifted up and grows strong and rejoicing when he passes through the Sign of Virgo.

The *countless interactions interknit* between Yod/Virgo and all the other letters (whose elements, planets, and signs stand in harmony *with* or hostility *to* Earth and Mercury) chart the ever-changing battle plans of the dream-wars of Yod.

Seize now the Rose of Yod and press its thorny stem against the upper blade of your sword so the beauty of the flower crowns and adorns the cross-guard of the hilt.

[WG assists Candidate if necessary.]

[Done.]

HT: *[Cont.]*
The dream of pain; the dream of pleasure. The battles of the letter *Yod* are never resolved while we dream . . . but only when we awaken.

[WG guides the Candidate to the Lamed/Libra point of the star.]

 [Heb: Lamed]

WG: *[Loudly shaking the Dodecahedron]*
All substance lives and struggles evermore

Through countless shapes continually at war,

By countless interactions interknit:

HT:

Behold the letter *Lamed*! To one who is awakened, *Lamed* is the monogram of pure God-consciousness. But for those who linger yet in dream, *Lamed* is an "Ox Goad" and alludes to "Work." The Mother Letter, Aleph, means "Ox," so Lamed (the Ox Goad) is the instrument that prods forward the immense life-force of Aleph. Furthermore, the Ox Goad serves to keep the forward motion balanced and straight, should it veer to the left or to the right.

In the dream of space-time, *Lamed* is the zodiac sign *Libra*, the Cardinal Sign of Air—Libra, who is ruled by beautiful, self-indulgent, and peace-loving Venus. Libra, where mature and stern disciplinarian Saturn is lifted up and grows strong and rejoicing when he passes through the Sign of Libra.

The *countless interactions interknit* between Lamed/Libra and all the other letters (whose elements, planets, and signs stand in harmony *with* or hostility *to* Air, Venus, and Saturn) chart the ever-changing battle plans of the dream-wars of Lamed.

Seize now the Rose of Lamed and press its thorny stem against the upper blade of your sword so the beauty of the flower crowns and adorns the cross-guard of the hilt.

[WG assists Candidate if necessary.]

[Done.]

HT: *[Cont.]*
The dream of pain; the dream of pleasure. The battles of the letter *Lamed* are never resolved while we dream . . . but only when we awaken.

[WG guides the Candidate to the Nun/Scorpio point of the star.]

 [Heb: Nun]

WG: *[Loudly shaking the Dodecahedron]*
All substance lives and struggles evermore

Through countless shapes continually at war,

By countless interactions interknit:

HT:
Behold the letter *Nun*! To one who is awakened, *Nun* is the monogram of pure God-consciousness. But for those who linger yet in dream, *Nun* is a "Fish" and alludes to "Walking" and "Motion." Fish are creatures of the sea and breed exuberantly. Out of the water, however, and when exposed to air, death swiftly claims them, and their flesh quickly decomposes with fiery heat that fertilizes the womb of earth with the nutrients that feed new life.

In the dream of space-time, *Nun* is the zodiac sign *Scorpio*, the Fixed Sign of Water—Scorpio, who is ruled by strong, active, and war-like Mars.

The *countless interactions interknit* between Nun/Scorpio and all the other letters (whose elements, planets, and signs stand in harmony *with* or hostility *to* Water and Mars) chart the ever-changing battle plans of the dream-wars of Nun.

Seize now the Rose of Nun and press its thorny stem against the upper blade of your sword so the beauty of the flower crowns and adorns the cross-guard of the hilt.

[WG assists Candidate if necessary.]

[Done.]

HT: *[Cont.]*
The dream of pain; the dream of pleasure. The battles of the letter *Nun* are never resolved while we dream . . . but only when we awaken.

[WG guides the Candidate to the Samekh/
Sagittarius point of the star.]

 [Heb: Samekh]

WG: *[Loudly shaking the Dodecahedron]*
All substance lives and struggles evermore

Through countless shapes continually at war,

By countless interactions interknit:

HT:
Behold the letter *Samekh*! To one who is awakened, *Samekh* is the mono-gram of pure God-consciousness. But for those who linger yet in dream, *Samekh* is a "Tent Pole" or "Prop" and alludes to the emotion of "Anger." A tent is a lifeless and empty skin until erected by its pole. Your body is an incoherent mass of organic material until supported and electrified by the scaffolding of your spine, brain, and nervous system. Samekh is the eternally arcing spark of consciousness that upholds and animates all forms.

In the dream of space-time, *Samekh* is the zodiac sign *Sagittarius*, the Mutable Sign of Fire—Sagittarius, who is ruled by benevolent, expansive, and philosophical Jupiter.

The *countless interactions interknit* between Samekh/Sagittarius and all the other letters (whose elements, planets, and signs stand in harmony *with* or hostility *to* Fire and Jupiter) chart the ever-changing battle plans of the dream-wars of Samekh.

Seize now the Rose of Samekh and press its thorny stem against the upper blade of your sword so the beauty of the flower crowns and adorns the cross-guard of the hilt.

[WG assists Candidate if necessary.]

[Done.]

HT: *[Cont.]*
The dream of pain; the dream of pleasure. The battles of the letter *Samekh* are never resolved while we dream . . . but only when we awaken.

[WG guides the Candidate to the Ayin/
Capricorn point of the star.]

  [Heb: Ayin]

WG: *[Loudly shaking the Dodecahedron]*
All substance lives and struggles evermore

Through countless shapes continually at war,

By countless interactions interknit:

HT:
Behold the letter *Ayin*. To one who is awakened, *Ayin* is the monogram of pure God-consciousness. But for those who linger yet in dream, *Ayin* is an "Eye" and alludes to "Laughter." Even though the letter *Heh* means "window" and represents the sense of "sight," the letter *Ayin* is the organ of the eye itself. Nothing is hidden from the all-seeing eye that is God-consciousness, and it is easy to imagine how the kaleidoscopic spectacle of illusions we call existence is profoundly amusing to the Great Eye. This same eye, by virtue of shape, is suggestive of both gates of life—the female yoni and the male meatus.

In the dream of space-time, *Ayin* is the zodiac sign *Capricorn*, the Cardinal Sign of Earth—Capricorn, who is ruled by the mature and stern disciplinarian Saturn. Capricorn, where the strong, active, and war-like Mars is lifted up and grows strong and rejoicing when he passes through the Sign of Capricorn.

The *countless interactions interknit* between Ayin/Capricorn and all the other letters (whose elements, planets, and signs stand in harmony *with* or hostility *to* Earth, Saturn, and Mars) chart the ever-changing battle plans of the dream-wars of Ayin.

Seize now the Rose of Ayin and press its thorny stem against the upper blade of your sword so the beauty of the flower crowns and adorns the cross-guard of the hilt.

[WG assists Candidate if necessary.]

[Done.]

HT: *[Cont.]*
The dream of pain; the dream of pleasure. The battles of the letter *Ayin* are never resolved while we dream . . . but only when we awaken.

*[WG guides the Candidate to the Tzaddi/
Aquarius point of the star.]*

 [Heb: Tzaddi]

WG: *[Loudly shaking the Dodecahedron]*
All substance lives and struggles evermore

Through countless shapes continually at war,

By countless interactions interknit:

HT:
Behold the letter *Tzaddi*. To one who is awakened, *Tzaddi* is the monogram of pure God-consciousness. But for those who linger yet in dream, *Tzaddi* is a "Hook" or "Fish Hook" (also words suggestive of "hunting," "lying-in-wait," and "capture") and alludes to the processes of "Thinking" and "Meditation." With Tzaddi, the awakening process is seen as a fishing expedition, where focused thought, meditation, and inspiration serve as the angling gear. But the process is mysterious and subtle; for both you and God are simultaneously *fish* and *fisherman*.

In the dream of space-time, *Tzaddi* is the zodiac sign *Aquarius*, the Fixed Sign of Air—Aquarius, who is ruled by the mature and stern disciplinarian Saturn.

The *countless interactions interknit* between Tzaddi/Aquarius and all the other letters (whose elements, planets, and signs stand in harmony *with* or hostility *to* Air and Saturn) chart the ever-changing battle plans of the dream-wars of Tzaddi.

Seize now the Rose of Tzaddi and press its thorny stem against the upper blade of your sword so the beauty of the flower crowns and adorns the cross-guard of the hilt.

[WG assists Candidate if necessary.]

[Done.]

HT: *[Cont.]*
The dream of pain; the dream of pleasure. The battles of the letter *Tzaddi* are never resolved while we dream . . . but only when we awaken.

[WG guides the Candidate to the Qoph/Pisces point of the star.]

 [Heb: Qoph]

WG: *[Loudly shaking the Dodecahedron]*
All substance lives and struggles evermore

Through countless shapes continually at war,

By countless interactions interknit:

HT:
Behold the letter *Qoph*! To one who is awakened, *Qoph* is the monogram of pure God-consciousness. But for those who linger yet in dream, *Qoph* is a "Back of the head" and alludes to "Sleep." The back of the head is a very primitive area of the brain, the part that remains active during sleep or when we are otherwise "unconscious"—a consciousness that seems very strange when we try to understand it with our rational mind.

In the dream of space-time, *Qoph* is the zodiac sign *Pisces*, the Mutable Sign of Water—Pisces, who is ruled by benevolent, expansive, and philosophical Jupiter—Pisces, where the beautiful, self-indulgent, and peace-loving Venus is lifted up and grows strong and rejoicing when she passes through the Sign of Pisces.

The *countless interactions interknit* between Qoph/Pisces and all the other letters (whose elements, planets, and signs stand in harmony *with* or hostility *to* Water, Jupiter, and Venus) chart the ever-changing battle plans of the dream-wars of Qoph.

Seize now the Rose of Qoph and press its thorny stem against the upper blade of your sword so the beauty of the flower crowns and adorns the cross-guard of the hilt.

[WG assists Candidate if necessary.]

[Done.]

HT: *[Cont.]*
The dream of pain; the dream of pleasure. The battles of the letter *Qoph* are never resolved while we dream . . . but only when we awaken.

HT: *[Cont.]*
Worthy Guide, I see that our Comrade-in-Arms has been wounded in battle and needs to dress her wounds and heal. See to it that she is properly cared for. Upon her return, she will collect the spoils of the War of Roses.

> *[WG escorts the Candidate back to the waiting area and, if necessary, helps clean, disinfect, and dress any scratches or cuts the Candidate might have incurred from the rose thorns.]*

> *[WG then returns to the Temple and helps HT place three floor cushions on the floorcloth as was done in the previous degrees.]*

III

PENETRATION OF THE TEMPLE OF THE TWELVE LETTERS

> *[WG collects Candidate in the waiting area and guides her to the outside of the Temple door (which is closed). WG instructs Candidate to knock loudly twelve times.]*

> *[Done. Knocks 4-4-4.]*

> *[HT goes to the door. He does not yet open it.]*

HT: *[Speaking loudly from inside the Temple door]*
Who knocks at the door of the Temple of the Twelve Simple Letters?

WG: *[Loudly answers from outside the Temple door]*
A Dear Friend and Comrade who has Illuminated our Temple and has heroically ennobled herself in the War of Roses. She has been tested and blooded and duly received in Our Holy Order. She now demands entrance to the *Temple of the Twelve Simple Letters* to be tempered by the Ordeal of the Twelve.

HT: *[From inside the Temple door]*
Does she volunteer of her own free will and accord to undergo such an ordeal?

> *[Even if the Candidate has heard the question, WG carefully repeats question.]*

WG: *[To Candidate]*
Do you volunteer of your own free will and accord to undergo such an ordeal?

> *[If Candidate agrees, WG encourages*
> *her to loudly answer "Yes."]*

CANDIDATE: *[From outside the Temple door]*
YES!

> *[Hearing the Candidate's affirmative answer,*
> *HT opens the door and greets Candidate at the*
> *threshold with a look of serious urgency.]*

HT:
I greet you at the threshold of the *Temple of the Twelve Simple Letters*! However, before you can properly penetrate the membrane of our sacred Temple, you must demonstrate to us and to yourself that you have distinguished yourself in battle. Worthy Guide, please instruct our Comrade how to properly give the *Sign*, *Grip*, and *Word* of the Third-Degree.

WG: *[Demonstrating for Candidate]*
The Third-Degree *Sign* is given as follows:

- Raise both hands in front of face, palms flat, facing each other, fingers pointing upwards, thumbs pointing at eyes.

- Clap hands once.

- Then give "thumbs-up" gesture with both hands (still at eye level). The twelve fingers needed for this gesture allude to the Twelve Simple Letters.

> *[Candidate repeats action.]*

WG: *[Cont.]*
The Third-Degree *Grip* (includes the exchange of the *Word*) is given as follows:

- First person raises right hand, palm forward (as if to invite a "high-five" congratulatory hand slap) and says, "Balance."

- Second person does the same and says, "Harmony."

- Both slap hands and say together, "Beauty."

- First person smiles and gives thumbs-up gesture with right hand.

- Second person smiles and gives thumbs-up gesture with right hand.

[WG exchanges Grip and Word with Candidate.]

HT:

Dear Friend and Comrade, these are the Signs and Tokens whereby one Third-Degree Initiate of Our Holy Order may know another. These actions may appear on the surface to be childish and whimsical. I assure you, however, the magical significance of these simple gestures and words is profound and powerful. Memorize them. Meditate upon them. You must prove proficient in their execution in order to gain admission to a Third-Degree Temple.

But more importantly, you most assuredly will be called upon to employ them as magic gestures that serve to open doors and unlock mysterious levels of consciousness in your own dreams and astral visions. They are in truth the secret Signs and Words that open up the next level of your own awakening.

I now invite you to take your seat in the Temple.

[HT and WG escort Candidate to her cushion on
the floorcloth and instruct her to be seated so she
may comfortably view the screen in the East.]

[HT and WG seat themselves in back and to each side of
the Candidate so they can speak unseen into her ears.]

IV

OPENING OF THE TWELVE GATES TO THE CITY

*[As in the Second-Degree ceremony, the Candidate will
undergo the meditation of "ghost images" of the Hebrew
letters. The Musician's role during this section is very
important and must be synchronized precisely to the
changes of images on the screen. These changes are a vitally
important aspect to the ritual because of the effects they
are designed to have on the Candidate's consciousness.[3]
All care must be taken to ensure the Candidate experience
the "floating ghost" optical phenomena of Hebrew
letters at the proper moment in the ceremony.]*

HT:

There are Twelve Gates to the City. For those trapped in the dream of eternal conflict, the Gates remain locked from within and without. Receive now the Twelve Keys. Unlock the Gates—and awaken.

MUSIC

Mid-range C held.

[Heb: Heh] ה

SLIDE # ?[4]

Large scarlet Heh against green background.

WG:

Gaze deeply at the Sacred Letter *Heh*. Fix your eyes upon it. On the fragmented battlefield of dream-life Heh is a Window . . .

SLIDE # ?

Large green Heh against scarlet background.

WG:

. . . but for you, it must be a Gate . . . one of the Twelve Gates of the City of God-consciousness.

....

SLIDE # ?

Total blackness.

....

[Pause.]

....

SLIDE # ?

Large scarlet Heh against green background.

....

[Pause.]

....

SLIDE # ?

*Slide changes to bright white; in doing so, creates the floating
green ghost image of Heh in the Candidate's brain.*

....

HT:

See now, with the eyes of your soul, the true color and image of Heh. Close
your eyes and implant it deep in the center of your brain, for it is the Key
that unlocks the First Gate of the City.

[Pause.]

....

MUSIC

Mid-range C# held.

....

[Heb: Vav] ו

....

SLIDE # ?

Large red-orange Vav against blue-green background.

....

WG:

Gaze deeply at the Sacred Letter *Vav*. Fix your eyes upon it. On the fragmented battlefield of dream-life Vav is a Nail . . .

....

SLIDE # ?

Large blue-green Vav against red-orange background.

....

WG:

. . . but for you, it must be a Gate . . . one of the Twelve Gates of the City of
God-consciousness.

....

SLIDE # ?

Total blackness.

....

[Pause.]

....

SLIDE # ?

Large red-orange Vav against blue-green background.

....

[Pause.]

....

SLIDE # ?

Slide changes to bright white; in doing so, creates the floating blue-green ghost image of Vav in the Candidate's brain.

....

HT:

See now, with the eyes of your soul, the true color and image of Vav. Close your eyes and implant it deep in the center of your brain, for it is the Key that unlocks the Second Gate of the City.

[Pause.]

....

MUSIC

Mid-range D held.

....

[Heb: Zain] ז

....

SLIDE # ?

Large orange Zain against blue background.

....

WG:

Gaze deeply at the Sacred Letter *Zain*. Fix your eyes upon it. On the fragmented battlefield of dream-life Zain is a Prop or a Tent Pole . . .

....

SLIDE # ?

Large blue Zain against orange background.

....

WG:

. . . but for you, it must be a Gate . . . one of the Twelve Gates of the City of God-consciousness.

··

SLIDE # ?

Total blackness.

··

[Pause.]

··

SLIDE # ?

Large orange Zain against blue background.

··

[Pause.]

··

SLIDE # ?

Slide changes to bright white; in doing so, creates the floating blue ghost image of Zain in the Candidate's brain.

··

HT:

See now, with the eyes of your soul, the true color and image of Zain. Close your eyes and implant it deep in the center of your brain, for it is the Key that unlocks the Third Gate of the City.

[Pause.]

··

MUSIC

Mid-range D⁺ held.

··

[Heb: Cheth] ח

··

SLIDE # ?

Large amber Cheth against indigo background.

··

WG:

Gaze deeply at the Sacred Letter *Cheth*. Fix your eyes upon it. On the fragmented battlefield of dream-life Cheth is a Fence or a Field . . .

··

SLIDE # ?

Large indigo Cheth against amber background.

··

WG:

. . . but for you, it must be a Gate . . . one of the Twelve Gates of the City of God-consciousness.

....

SLIDE # ?

Total blackness.

....

[Pause.]

....

SLIDE # ?

Large amber Cheth against indigo background.

....

[Pause.]

....

SLIDE # ?

Slide changes to bright white; in doing so, creates the floating indigo ghost image of Cheth in the Candidate's brain.

....

HT:

See now, with the eyes of your soul, the true color and image of Cheth. Close your eyes and implant it deep in the center of your brain, for it is the Key that unlocks the Fourth Gate of the City.

[Pause.]

....

MUSIC

Mid-range E held.

....

[Heb: Teth] ט

....

SLIDE # ?

Large greenish-yellow Teth against crimson background.

....

WG:

Gaze deeply at the Sacred Letter *Teth*. Fix your eyes upon it. On the fragmented battlefield of dream-life Teth is a Serpent . . .

....

SLIDE # ?

Large crimson Teth against greenish-yellow background.

....

WG:

. . . but for you, it must be a Gate . . . one of the Twelve Gates of the City of God-consciousness.

··

SLIDE # ?

Total blackness.

··

[Pause.]

··

SLIDE # ?

Large greenish-yellow Teth against crimson background.

··

[Pause.]

··

SLIDE # ?

*Slide changes to bright white; in doing so, creates the floating
crimson ghost image of Teth in the Candidate's brain.*

··

HT:

See now, with the eyes of your soul, the true color and image of Teth. Close
your eyes and implant it deep in the center of your brain, for it is the Key
that unlocks the Fifth Gate of the City.

[Pause.]

··

MUSIC

Mid-range F held.

··

י

[Heb: Yod]

··

SLIDE # ?

Large yellowish-green Yod against greenish-yellow background.

··

WG:

Gaze deeply at the Sacred Letter *Yod*. Fix your eyes upon it. On the fragmented battlefield of dream-life Yod is a Hand . . .

··

SLIDE # ?

Large greenish-yellow Yod against yellowish-green background.

··

WG:

. . . but for you, it must be a Gate . . . one of the Twelve Gates of the City of
God-consciousness.

··

SLIDE # ?

Total blackness.

··

[Pause.]

··

SLIDE # ?

Large yellowish-green Yod against greenish-yellow background.

··

[Pause.]

··

SLIDE # ?

Slide changes to bright white; in doing so, creates the floating greenish-yellow ghost image of Yod in the Candidate's brain.

··

HT:

See now, with the eyes of your soul, the true color and image of Yod. Close your eyes and implant it deep in the center of your brain, for it is the Key that unlocks the Sixth Gate of the City.

[Pause.]

··

MUSIC:

Mid-range F♯ held.

··

[Heb: Lamed]

··

SLIDE # ?

Large emerald-green Lamed against violet background.

··

WG:

Gaze deeply at the Sacred Letter *Lamed*. Fix your eyes upon it. On the fragmented battlefield of dream-life Lamed is an Ox Goad . . .

··

SLIDE # ?

Large violet Lamed against emerald-green background.

··

WG:

. . . but for you, it must be a Gate . . . one of the Twelve Gates of the City of God-consciousness.

....

SLIDE # ?

Total blackness.

....

[Pause.]

....

SLIDE # ?

Large emerald-green Lamed against violet background.

....

[Pause.]

....

SLIDE # ?

Slide changes to bright white; in doing so, creates the floating violet ghost image of Lamed in the Candidate's brain.

....

HT:

See now, with the eyes of your soul, the true color and image of Lamed. Close your eyes and implant it deep in the center of your brain, for it is the Key that unlocks the Seventh Gate of the City.

[Pause.]

....

MUSIC

Mid-range G held.

....

[Heb: Nun] נ

....

SLIDE # ?

Large greenish-blue Nun against reddish-orange background.

....

WG:

Gaze deeply at the Sacred Letter *Nun*. Fix your eyes upon it. On the fragmented battlefield of dream-life Nun is a Fish . . .

....

SLIDE # ?

Large reddish-orange Nun against greenish-blue background.

....

WG:

. . . but for you, it must be a Gate . . . one of the Twelve Gates of the City of God-consciousness.

··

SLIDE # ?

Total blackness.

··

[Pause.]

··

SLIDE # ?

Large greenish-blue Nun against reddish-orange background.

··

[Pause.]

··

SLIDE # ?

Slide changes to bright white; in doing so, creates the floating reddish-orange ghost image of Nun in the Candidate's brain.

··

HT:

See now, with the eyes of your soul, the true color and image of Nun. Close your eyes and implant it deep in the center of your brain, for it is the Key that unlocks the Eighth Gate of the City.

[Pause.]

··

MUSIC

Mid-range G held.

··

[Heb: Samekh] ס

··

SLIDE # ?

Large blue Samekh against orange background.

··

WG:

Gaze deeply at the Sacred Letter *Samekh*. Fix your eyes upon it. On the fragmented battlefield of dream-life Samekh is a Prop or a Tent Pole . . .

··

SLIDE # ?

Large orange Samekh against blue background.

··

WG:

. . . but for you, it must be a Gate . . . one of the Twelve Gates of the City of God-consciousness.

···

SLIDE # ?

Total blackness.

···

[Pause.]

···

SLIDE # ?

Large blue Samekh against orange background.

···

[Pause.]

···

SLIDE # ?

Slide changes to bright white; in doing so, creates the floating orange ghost image of Samekh in the Candidate's brain.

···

HT:

See now, with the eyes of your soul, the true color and image of Samekh. Close your eyes and implant it deep in the center of your brain, for it is the Key that unlocks the Ninth Gate of the City.

[Pause.]

···

· MUSIC

Mid-range A held.

···

[Heb: Ayin] עי

···

SLIDE # ?

Large indigo Ayin against deep amber background.

···

WG:

Gaze deeply at the Sacred Letter *Ayin*. Fix your eyes upon it. On the fragmented battlefield of dream-life Ayin is an Eye . . .

···

SLIDE # ?

Large deep amber Ayin against indigo background.

···

WG:

. . . but for you, it must be a Gate . . . one of the Twelve Gates of the City of God-consciousness.

....

SLIDE # ?

Total blackness.

....

[Pause.]

....

SLIDE # ?

Large indigo Ayin against deep amber background.

....

[Pause.]

....

SLIDE # ?

*Slide changes to bright white; in doing so, creates the floating
deep amber ghost image of Ayin in the Candidate's brain.*

....

HT:

See now, with the eyes of your soul, the true color and image of Ayin. Close
your eyes and implant it deep in the center of your brain, for it is the Key
that unlocks the Tenth Gate of the City.

[Pause.]

....

MUSIC

Mid-range B♭ held.

....

[Heb: Tzaddi] צ

....

SLIDE # ?

Large violet Tzaddi against yellow background.

....

WG:

Gaze deeply at the Sacred Letter *Tzaddi*. Fix your eyes upon it. On the fragmented battlefield of dream-life Tzaddi is a Fishhook . . .

....

SLIDE # ?

Large yellow Tzaddi against violet background.

....

WG:

. . . but for you, it must be a Gate . . . one of the Twelve Gates of the City of
God-consciousness.

....

SLIDE # ?

Total blackness.

....

[Pause.]

....

SLIDE # ?

Large violet Tzaddi against yellow background.

....

[Pause.]

....

SLIDE # ?

*Slide changes to bright white; in doing so, creates the floating
yellow ghost image of Tzaddi in the Candidate's brain.*

....

HT:

See now, with the eyes of your soul, the true color and image of Tzaddi.
Close your eyes and implant it deep in the center of your brain, for it is the
Key that unlocks the Eleventh Gate of the City.

[Pause.]

....

MUSIC

Mid-range B held.

....

[Heb: Qoph] קֿ

....

SLIDE # ?

Large crimson Qoph against yellow-green background.

....

WG:

Gaze deeply at the Sacred Letter *Qoph*. Fix your eyes upon it. On the fragmented battlefield of dream-life Qoph is the Back of the Head . . .

....

SLIDE # ?

Large yellow-green Qoph against crimson background.

....

WG:

. . . but for you, it must be a Gate . . . one of the Twelve Gates of the City of
God-consciousness.

....

SLIDE # ?

Total blackness.

....

[Pause.]

....

SLIDE # ?

Large crimson Qoph against yellow-green background.

....

[Pause.]

*Slide changes to bright white; in doing so, creates the floating
yellow-green ghost image of Qoph in the Candidate's brain.*

....

HT:

See now, with the eyes of your soul, the true color and image of Qoph. Close
your eyes and implant it deep in the center of your brain, for it is the Key
that unlocks the Twelfth and final Gate of the City.

....

SLIDE # ?

Total blackness.

....

HT: *[Cont.]*

Arise, O Master of the Twelve Letters, and receive a sacred token of your
Degree.

*[All rise. WG removes the cushions, retrieves
the large Presentation Dodecahedron[5] from its
place of concealment, and hands it to HT.]*

V

PRESENTATION OF THE DODECAHEDRON, THE THIRD-DEGREE CUBE, AND THE ROBE

....

MUSIC

*MUSICIAN plays the deepest, lowest A note possible.
Ideally, this A note should be of such a low frequency
that it is nearly inaudible . . . a background hum. This
note is sustained until the Closing ceremony begins.*

....

HT:
It gives me the greatest pleasure to present you with this *toy.*

[HT hands new Master the Dodecahedron.]

HT: *[Cont.]*
It is called a Dodecahedron, one of the five Platonic Solids. It has twelve faces, which, as you can see, are inscribed with the Twelve Simple Letters of the Hebrew alphabet, the numbers they represent, zodiac signs, and other information pertaining to the Simple Letters.

But there is more to your new toy than meets the eye. Please shake it.

[New Master shakes the Dodecahedron.]

HT: *[Cont.]*
As the hard shell of an egg conceals and protects the delicate, fertilized life within, so do the twelve combatant Simple Letters form a shell around the subtler levels of consciousness from which they condensed.

What you hear inside your Dodecahedron Egg is your Second-Degree Cube of Double Letters, clamoring like planets that careen back and forth within the walls of the zodiac.

And piercing the six sides of your Second-Degree Cube, giving it its form, and creating Time and Space, is your First-Degree pipe cleaner toy of Three Mother Letters.

WG:
And Tav? Honored Teacher, where in the rattling Egg is the Letter *Tav*?

HT:
Worthy Guide, it is hidden. Tav dwells silently in the very midst of all . . .

....
MUSIC

When HT says the word midst, *MUSICIAN continues*
to play the deepest, lowest A note possible, but brings up
the volume to a dramatic (but not painful) rumble.
....

HT: *[Cont.]*
. . . as the most *visible* manifestation of existence, and the most *invisible* source of Being.

Tav is hidden. The Secret Primal Center, the Point—the silence that is the source of the "rattle."

....

Music stops.
....

HT: *[Cont.]*
Your Third-Degree toy is a geometric model of the cosmos of creation; revealing in form the three great steps of the descent of consciousness; from the absolute singularity of *the Primal Center godhead*; through the dream limitations of space and time (*the Three Mother Letters*); through the dream of separation and duality (*the Seven Double Letters*); to the dream-wars of observable existence (*the Twelve Simple Letters*). This is the world in which the infinite clothes itself with the finite; where the One dreams it is the many; where *All substance lives and struggles evermore—Through countless shapes continually at war—By countless interactions interknit*; a world whose dramas have so distracted you . . . that you have forgotten you are God.

[WG fetches the Third-Degree Cube (displaying the twelve signs of the zodiac along the edges . . . the cube that sat on the table in the waiting area) and hands it to HT.]

HT: *[Presents Third-Degree Cube to Candidate.]*
And because your Second-Degree Cube is forever sealed inside your new Dodecahedron toy (and none of us enjoy losing a toy), it pleases me to present you with a special Third-Degree Cube, which is just like your Second-Degree Cube with the Twelve Letters and zodiac signs added to the edges.

[WG fetches the Candidate's new black robe and hands it to HT.]

HT: *[Presents robe to Candidate.]*
I now present you with the Robe of Our Holy Order, which we hope you will wear with pleasure during all our ceremonies and during your personal practices and meditations. The robe is black, to remind you that you are the Primal Center of All. During the First- and Second-Degree Initiation ceremonies, we wear the hood down. For the Third-Degree work, we wear the hood up.

HT:
And now, Friends and Comrades, be pleased to assist me to close the Temple of the Third-Degree.

VI

CLOSING CEREMONY

*[Newly initiated Candidate stands in the West of the
Temple and observes and follows directions.]*

HT: *[Claps 4-4-4.]*
Friends and Comrades, assist me to close this Temple in the Third-Degree.

*[WG joins HT in the East where they exchange the
Sign, Grip, and Word of the Third-Degree.]*

*[HT turns to the new initiate and they exchange the
Sign, Grip, and Word of the Third-Degree.]*

HT:
The Sign is made. The Grip is given. The Word is Spoken. I declare the
Temple Closed in the Third-Degree.

HT: *[Claps 4-4-4.]*

WG: *[Claps 4-4-4.]*

HT: *[Claps twenty-two times, 7-7-7-1.]*
Conception is accomplished. The seeds are alive. All twenty-two letters are
now implanted deep in your awakening soul; seeds that are now growing
with their own life force. Continue to nurture them with your persistent,
loving attention. Do this and you will surely give birth to your awakened self.

VII

PRESENTATION OF PORTFOLIO

[WG fetches the Third-Degree Portfolio and hands it to HT.]

HT: *[Presents Portfolio to Candidate.]*
I present you with your Third-Degree Study Portfolio. It contains a complete
copy of the Initiation Ceremony you have just experienced. Please recall
what was said to you on the previous occasions, that you should continually
study, memorize, and rehearse it in the mental Temple of your imagination.

WG:
Honored Teacher. We have all labored long and hard. Is the Great Work nothing but ordeals and lectures and wearing robes and strutting around in the dark? I, for one, am in need of refreshment.

WG: *[speaking to the new Initiate]*
Sister, are these your sentiments also? Are you in need of refreshment?

CANDIDATE:
YES!

HT:
Then so be it. We have a pleasant surprise for you. As on the occasion of your First-Degree Initiation, we have scheduled a celebratory banquet in your honor. After the festivities, we want you to return to your room and relax, bathe, and perhaps even take a well-deserved nap. We will meet again in the Temple shortly before midnight, to commune as Masters for one final meditation. Please wear your robe and bring your journal and a pen or pencil with you. You will need them.

> *[All retire to the Banquet Hall for dinner and entertainment.*
> *As it is an occasion of great merriment, this celebration*
> *can be joined by any other Third-Degree Initiates who*
> *wish to attend. After the feast all retire to rest, returning*
> *in their Third-Degree robes to the Temple at midnight.]*

VIII

MIDNIGHT MEDITATION ASCENDING THE TWENTY-TWO PATHS OF THE TREE OF LIFE

> *[The Temple remains as it was at the conclusion of the Third-*
> *Degree Initiation, with the exception of three floor cushions*
> *that have been set out and arranged as in the previous*
> *initiations. Other Third-Degree witnesses, if there be any,*
> *may seat themselves on either side of the floorcloth.]*

> *[The Temple is illuminated only by the ten candles*
> *of the candelabra and the Menorah.]*

> *[The screen is black and remains so until near the end of*
> *the meditation when it simply changes to bright white.]*

[There are no musical cues played by the Musician.]

[All wear robes (hoods up) and meet unceremoniously at the Temple door at midnight.]

[HT and WG escort Candidate to her cushion on the floorcloth and instruct her to be seated so she may comfortably view the blackened screen in the East. Other Third-Degree witnesses, if there be any, sit on either side of the floorcloth.]

[HT and WG seat themselves in back and to each side of the Candidate so they can speak unseen into her ears.]

....

SLIDE # ?

Blank black.

....

HT:

You see before you a blank screen—totally black—because this meditation will be projected entirely upon the inner screen of your mind.

I am sure you are familiar with the famous Qabalistic figure called *The Tree of Life*. (It is the subject of the reference works assigned for your study.) The Tree of Life is an attempt to represent in lines and circles and words and colors the opening words of the *Sepher Yezirah, The Book on Creation*:

> *God . . . created the Universe in thirty-two mysterious paths of wisdom . . . They consist of a decade out of nothing and of twenty-two fundamental letters.*[6]

The "decade out of nothing" are the ten Sephiroth (or major levels of descending consciousness spanning the spectrum between God-consciousness [#1] and your consciousness [#10]).

The "twenty-two fundamental letters" are those of the sacred Hebrew alphabet that connect the Sephiroth like twenty-two highly specialized facets of *intelligence* that (like electrical transformers) step up or step down the consciousness frequencies between the Sephiroth they connect. The descriptive names of the Intelligences are included on the three Tables in your Portfolios. Their mysterious descriptions are itemized in traditional Qabalistic texts, an example of which is included in your Third-Degree Portfolio.[7]

During this meditation, we will practice raising our consciousness step by step back up the ladder of consciousness. We will start at the very bottom paths of the Tree and work our way all the way to the top. Each Path has hundreds of Qabalistic Correspondences that are associated with a particular level of consciousness. For tonight's meditation, we will only work with three:

- Musical Note

- Color

- Archetypal visual images suggested by the Tarot card associated with the Path

This is a guided meditation, so you'll need to use your very best powers of imagination. So, while we are imagining things, we may as well make them pleasant and delightful. At each step of our journey, I will ask you to visualize yourself being kissed by the most beautiful angel or divine spirit you can imagine. This kiss will trigger the next awakening.

At each step, we will start by forcefully intoning the sound of the letter three times (on the proper musical note). Don't worry. The Worthy Guide has the pitch and will lead us in chanting the proper note.

Then, I will say a few words about the level of the Tree of Life we are visiting . . . then we shall all be silent for a few moments. I'll try not to say too much or try to lead your vision. In the moments of silence, I want you to just relax and simply observe the thoughts and images that come to your mind. You have your journal and pencil at hand, so you can write down short notes about what you saw, heard, and felt during those moments of silence. Remember. This is your skrying session—your vision. There is no right thing to see and no wrong thing to see.

If you are ready, take a few relaxing breaths and close your eyes.

Malkuth

HT:
Let's imagine you are standing in front of a small house.

You enter the front door of the house and find yourself in a black room.

To your left is an opened door to a room that is painted reddish-green; to your right is an opened door to a room that is painted brownish-green. Directly in front of you is an opened door to a room that is painted very, very dark green. It is almost black.

Directly above you is an opening in the ceiling. The opening is just wide enough for you to squeeze your body through, if you could only fly up and enter it. It is very, very dark up there, but you can hear strange and beautiful music coming from that opening above you. You want to rise up and enter into the blackness of the opening in the ceiling. As we chant, imagine yourself kissing your Angel and rising up and into the darkness.

Path of Tav

[WG blows A on the pitch pipe and leads the chant:]

Thahhhhhhh—Thahhhhhhh—Thahhhhhhh.[8]

HT:

Imagine yourself rising up and squeezing through the dark opening in the ceiling. Once you are inside, you see where the beautiful music is coming from—four magical creatures, a Lion, an Eagle, a Bull, and a beautiful Angel. They stand alongside a large oval mirror that is as tall as your own body. The mirror is shining a deep, dark indigo color. You realize the mirror is the center of the *entire universe* and in it you see the full image of yourself reflected.

Be still for a moment and observe what goes through your mind when you look into the mirror.

[Pause.]

If you need to write down a note, please do so now. Then close your eyes again.

[Pause.]

Now look again into the mirror while we chant. Again, imagine yourself kissing your Angel.

Path of Shin

[WG blows C on the pitch pipe and leads the chant:]

Shahhhhhhh—Shahhhhhhh—Shahhhhhhh.

HT:

The color of the mirror has now changed to a deep scarlet red. You see flames in the redness, but you are not afraid of being burned. You begin to feel that the flames are somehow helping you to wake up. You see yourself coming to life in the reflection in the mirror.

Be still for a moment, as you feel yourself being born in fire like a Phoenix. Now just observe what goes through your mind when you look into the mirror.

[Pause.]

If you need to write down a note, please do so now. Then close your eyes again.

[Pause.]

Now look again into the mirror while we chant. Again, imagine yourself kissing your Angel.

Path of Resh

[WG blows D on the pitch pipe and leads the chant:]

Rahhhhhhh—Rahhhhhhh—Rahhhhhhh.

HT:
The color of the mirror has now changed to a beautiful orange. In the very center of the mirror, you see the Sun blazing a brilliant golden orange. As you look at the Sun, you can still see your own reflection in the mirror. It's as though the Sun is shining from your own face and head. Around you, hear the music of the laughter of two children. You have the feeling that you have awakened to become the person you always wanted to be.

Now be still for a moment and feel the warm life of the sunshine upon your face. Just observe what goes through your mind as you continue to look into the mirror.

[Pause.]

If you need to write down a note, please do so now. Then close your eyes again.

[Pause.]

Now look again into the mirror while we chant. Again, imagine being kissed by your Angel.

Path of Qoph

[WG blows B on the pitch pipe and leads the chant:]

Quahhhhhhh—Quahhhhhhh—Quahhhhhhh.

HT:
The color of the mirror now changes to a reddish purple. In the center of the mirror, you see a strange image of the Moon. Part of it is a pale, slim crescent moon, but you can also see the rest of the sphere . . . it is blood-red. Now you begin to also see your own reflection in the mirror . . . but something is very weird. You are looking at the reflection of the *back of your body* . . . . The Moon seems to cover the *back of your head* instead of your face! You feel strange, and sleepy, and a bit uneasy. All around, you hear the howling of dogs or wolves.

Be still for a moment, and drink in the strange beauty of the scene. Just observe what goes through your mind as you continue to look into the mirror.

[Pause.]

If you need to write down a note, please do so now. Then close your eyes again.

[Pause.]

Now look again into the mirror while we chant, and imagine your Angel kissing you sweetly.

Path of Tzaddi

[WG blows A# on the pitch pipe and leads the chant:]

Tzahhhhhhh—Tzahhhhhhh—Tzahhhhhhh.

HT:

The color of the mirror now changes to a beautiful violet. The moon has disappeared completely from the mirror and now you see a beautiful, star-filled night sky dominated by one enormous star. You feel as if these stars have caught you like a fish and rescued you from the weird confusion of the Moon world. You now feel calm, centered, and at peace. You see yourself in the mirror closing your eyes and meditating on the vastness of space, as if all the stars were your brothers and sisters in the body of a Great Mother Star Goddess.

Be still for a moment and feel at home among the stars. Just observe what goes through your mind as you continue to look into the mirror.

[Pause.]

If you need to write down a note, please do so now. Then close your eyes again.

[Pause.]

Now look again into the mirror while we chant. Again, imagine yourself kissing your Angel.

Path of Peh

[WG blows C on the pitch pipe and leads the chant:]

Pahhhhhhh—Pahhhhhhh—Pahhhhhhh.

HT:

The color of the mirror now changes to a bright scarlet red You are startled by a blinding flash of lightning, followed by a loud clap of thunder. The mirror shakes so much you think it will shatter. You see your reflection standing in the mirror, but it appears that your body has been shaken so badly that it is crumbling to the ground like a stone tower struck by lightning. It looks terrible, but you are thrilled and excited, as if all the useless things in your life are being destroyed and thrown away.

Now be still for a moment and enjoy the mad exhilaration of this divine destruction . . . . Now just observe what goes through your mind, as you continue to look into the mirror.

[Pause.]

If you need to write down a note, please do so now. Then close your eyes again.

[Pause.]

Now look again into the mirror, while we chant. Again, imagine yourself kissing your Angel.

Path of Ayin

[WG blows A on the pitch pipe and leads the chant:]

Oyahhhhhhh—Oyahhhhhhh—Oyahhhhhhh.

HT:
The color of the mirror now changes to a dark indigo, and in the middle of the mirror, you see your own face reflected . . . but your face has become terrible and ugly. You have two horns growing from your head and your face is covered with a shaggy beard. As terrible as you look, you are not frightened. In fact, you laugh at the thought you can look so terrible and still be who you are. You think it would be fun scaring people who are too frightened to see the real YOU.

Be still for a moment and observe what goes through your mind, as you continue to look into the mirror.

[Pause.]

If you need to write down a note, please do so now. Then close your eyes again.

[Pause.]

Now look again into the mirror while we chant. Again, imagine yourself kissing your Angel.

Path of Samekh

[WG blows G# on the pitch pipe and leads the chant:]

Sahhhhhhh—Sahhhhhhh—Sahhhhhhh.

HT:

The color of the mirror now changes to a bright blue and you see your own reflection. Above your head bends a beautiful rainbow. It brings out the color in your eye. At your feet stand two fantastic creatures—a huge Red Eagle and beautiful White Lion. You hold a flaming torch in your right hand and a chalice of water in your left hand. Now touch the Red Eagle with the flame of your torch, and pour the water on the head of the White Lion. The fire makes the water hiss and steam, and the steam fills the mirror with all the colors of the rainbow.

Now be still for a moment and bathe yourself in the rainbow . . . feel yourself in the mist . . . now just observe what goes through your mind as you continue to look into the mirror.

[Pause.]

If you need to write down a note, please do so now. Then close your eyes again.

[Pause.]

Now look again into the mirror while we chant. Again, imagine yourself being kissed by your Angel.

Path of Nun

[WG blows G on the pitch pipe and leads the chant:]

Nahhhhhhh—Nahhhhhhh—Nahhhhhhh.

HT:

Now the color of the mirror changes to a bright green-blue, and your reflection in the mirror becomes the skeleton of Death. But you aren't afraid, because you see all around your reflection millions of tiny silver fishes darting this way and that. You also see eggs and embryos and fetuses of unborn humans and other living creatures. It is very beautiful, and you feel at peace to realize all life comes from this death, and that death is just part of the cycle of your existence. You feel like you are cradled in the dark, warm, moist womb of a great secret.

Bask for a moment in that unspoken mystery, and observe what goes through your mind as you continue to look into the mirror.

[Pause.]

If you need to write down a note, please do so now. Then close your eyes again.

[Pause.]

Now look again into the mirror while we chant. Again, imagine yourself kissing your Angel.

Path of Mem

[WG blows G$^{\#}$ on the pitch pipe and leads the chant:]

Mahhhhhhh—Mahhhhhhh—Mahhhhhhh.

HT:
Now the color of the magic mirror changes to a pale blue, and you are surprised to see the reflection of your body is upside down in the mirror. You don't feel like you are upside down, but there you are! For a moment, you are unsure if it is you or the entire universe that has flipped. This image soon disappears, and the mirror is filled with the vista of an infinitely deep ocean of still water. Try to feel yourself suspended upside down in the calm vastness of this sea as you quietly observe what goes through your mind as you continue to look into the mirror.

[Pause.]

If you need to write down a note, please do so now. Then close your eyes again.

[Pause.]

Gaze again into the mirror while we chant. Again, imagine yourself kissing your Angel.

Path of Lamed

[WG blows F$^{\#}$ on the pitch pipe and leads the chant:]

Lahhhhhhh—Lahhhhhhh—Lahhhhhhh.

HT:
The color of the mirror now changes to bright emerald green and you find yourself walking, step by step, along a very narrow green rope. The rope is

stretched tight between two trees. One tree is golden yellow in color and the other is red. You are balanced on the rope trying to carefully walk from the yellow tree to the red tree. You carefully balance yourself as you put one foot in front of the other until you finally safely reach the red tree.

That was easy to do, wasn't it? After all, anything is possible in a vision. But pause for a moment and try to remember the feeling of that hidden force inside you that kept you balanced—the force that compelled you to move forward on that tightrope. Try to capture that force, while you again observe what goes through your mind.

[Pause.]

If you need to write down a note, please do so now. Then close your eyes again.

[Pause.]

Now look again into the mirror while we chant. Again, imagine yourself kissing your Angel.

Path of Kaph

[WG blows B♭ on the pitch pipe and leads the chant:]

Kahhhhhhh—Kahhhhhhh—Kahhhhhhh.

HT:

The color of the mirror now changes to bright violet. At first you cannot see your own reflection because the mirror is filled with the image of a large wheel that spins counterclockwise. Situated around the wheel at the top and bottom corners of the mirror are the same four magical creatures you saw at the beginning of the meditation—a Lion, an Eagle, a Bull, and a beautiful Angel. On the rim of the wheel you see three other creatures, but it is hard to see what they are because the wheel is spinning so fast. When you look into the very center of the wheel . . . the hub . . . you see that the wheel is not moving at all. And there, in the very center of that motionless hub, you now clearly see *your own reflection.*

Enjoy the thrill of being the still and motionless hum, as the chaotic universe revolves around you. Observe what goes through your mind as the wheel turns.

[Pause.]

If you need to write down a note, please do so now. Then close your eyes again.

[Pause.]

Now look again into the mirror while we chant. Again, imagine yourself kissing your Angel.

Path of Yod

[WG blows F on the pitch pipe and leads the chant:]

Yahhhhhhh—Yahhhhhhh—Yahhhhhhh.

HT:
Now the color of the mirror changes to yellowish-green, and once again you see your own full reflection in the mirror. However, even though you are facing your reflection in the mirror, your image is in profile. Try as you may, you can only see the left half of your face and body. You are standing all alone on the top of a mountain and you hold a little lamp in your hand. Even though it is small, it is very bright, and it illuminates the entire world below you. Now you see that the flame in your lamp is the *Sun*. You feel oddly comfortable being all alone and silent. All of your joy comes out of your *lamp* . . . and it's your joy to give your light to the world.

Feel that solitary joy as you observe what goes through your mind.

[Pause.]

If you need to write down a note, please do so now. Then close your eyes again.

[Pause.]

Now look again into the mirror while we chant. Again, imagine your Angel kissing you. This kiss is full of ardor and surprises and thrills you with a new level of passion.

Path of Teth

[WG blows E on the pitch pipe and leads the chant:]

Tahhhhhhh—Tahhhhhhh—Tahhhhhhh.

HT:
The color of the mirror now changes to a warm greenish yellow and you hear the sound of a mighty lion roaring. The roar sounds as if it is coming from your own chest and heart. You have the uncontrollable urge to catch that roaring lion and ride madly on its back throughout the universe. Imagine for a moment that you are doing just that! Take note of where the lion takes you and what you experience.

[Pause.]

If you need to write down a note, please do so now. Then close your eyes again.

[Pause.]

Now look again into the mirror while we chant. Again, imagine yourself kissing your Angel.

Path of Cheth

[WG blows D on the pitch pipe and leads the chant:]*

Hcahhhhhh—Hcahhhhhhh—Hcahhhhhhh.

HT:
The color of the mirror has now changed to a beautiful bright amber. For a moment, it looks like the color is coming from the Sun, which shines brightly from the center of the mirror. Now you see yourself standing *behind* the Sun. Your body is covered in beautiful armor and you hold in your hands a golden cup. The Sun, and all the light, is shining from within the cup. You sense that all the life in the universe . . . everything that ever lived or will ever live . . . is in that Cup of Sunlight. You feel yourself to be a magical Knight, and that it is your sacred duty to deliver this precious cup to the Queen of Heaven. Now you see that you are standing in a beautiful Chariot and it is pulled by two sphinxes, one black and one white.

Be still now for a moment and observe what goes through your mind as you continue to look into the mirror and this glorious sight.

[Pause.]

If you need to write down a note, please do so now. Then close your eyes again.

[Pause.]

Now look again into the mirror while we chant. This time, imagine your Angel kisses you tenderly like Queen of Heaven might kiss her lover Knight.

Now look again into the mirror while we chant. Again, imagine yourself kissing your Angel.

Path of Zain

[WG blows D on the pitch pipe and leads the chant:]

Zahhhhhhh—Zahhhhhhh—Zahhhhhhh.

HT:

The color in the mirror has changed to a bright orange. This time you clearly see your reflection in the mirror, but you are *not* alone—in fact, there are *three of you*. To your left stands a beautiful, soft, and feminine version of yourself. She holds on to your left arm and is trying to *kiss* you on your check. On your right stands a very handsome, rugged, and masculine version of yourself who tries to kiss you on the other cheek. You feel you must decide which you prefer. Perhaps each is the correct choice.

Pause for a moment and think about that choice . . . then observe what goes through your mind as you continue to look into the mirror and ponder your choice.

[Pause.]

If you need to write down a note, please do so now. Then close your eyes again.

[Pause.]

Now look again into the mirror while we chant. Again, imagine yourself kissed by your Angel.

Path of Vav

[WG blows C# on the pitch pipe and leads the chant:]

Vahhhhhhh—Vahhhhhhh—Vahhhhhhh.

HT:

Now the color in the mirror changes to a bright red-orange. Again, see your reflection. This time you are dressed as a very important Priest or Holy person. There are two monks kneeling in front of you to serve you. You don't look at them, because you are deeply entranced in serene meditation. You point to your ear, as if to say, "Listen to the voice of your soul."

Be still for a moment. Lose yourself in that deep trance. Observe how it feels and what goes through your mind.

[Pause.]

If you need to write down a note, please do so now. Then close your eyes again.

[Pause.]

Now look again into the mirror while we chant. Again, imagine yourself kissing your Angel.

Path of Heh

[WG blows C on the pitch pipe and leads the chant:]

Hahhhhhhh—Hahhhhhhh—Hahhhhhhh.

HT:
Now the color in the mirror changes to scarlet red and you see yourself seated on a throne as a mighty Emperor. Your head is turned so you can only see half your face in the mirror. Think for a moment . . . . What is the kingdom that you oversee with the eye we see in the mirror, and what kingdom do you oversee with the eye that is hidden?

Now be still for a moment and observe what goes through your mind as you continue to look into the mirror.

[Pause.]

If you need to write down a note, please do so now. Then close your eyes again.

[Pause.]

Now look again into the mirror while we chant. Again, imagine yourself kissing your Angel. This time, however, the kiss feels as warm and loving as a mother's kiss.

Path of Daleth

[WG blows F# on the pitch pipe and leads the chant:]

Dahhhhhhh—Dahhhhhhh—Dahhhhhhh.

HT:
Now the color in the mirror changes again . . . this time to a beautiful emerald green. You see yourself seated again on a throne; only this time you are a great Queen in a beautiful green dress. You are sitting in a garden full of flowers. You smile as you realize that you are pregnant with the entire cosmos and that this is the garden of your divine LOVE.

Linger for a moment in this happy garden and observe what goes through your mind as you feel the ecstasy of this cosmic and universal love.

[Pause.]

If you need to write down a note, please do so now. Then close your eyes again.

[Pause.]

Now look again into the mirror while we chant. Again, imagine yourself kissing your Angel.

Path of Gimel

[WG blows G# on the pitch pipe and leads the chant:]

Gahhhhhhh—Gahhhhhhh—Gahhhhhhh.

HT:
Now the color in the mirror changes to a dark blue. You still see yourself seated, but now you are a beautiful YOUNG woman, a Virgin. You wear the Crescent Moon in your hair—you don't speak a word, but your silence tells the story of all creation! You hold a book against your breast—the secret of the universe is in that book and only you can protect that secret. But you will share the secret with all who can hear it in your *silence*.

Linger in the silence and observe what goes through your mind.

[Pause.]

If you need to write down a note, please do so now. Then close your eyes again.

[Pause.]

Now look again into the mirror while we chant. Again, imagine yourself kissing your Angel.

Path of Beth

[WG blows E on the pitch pipe and leads the chant:]

Bahhhhhhh—Bahhhhhhh—Bahhhhhhh.

HT:
Now the color in the mirror changes to a bright yellow and you see yourself standing behind a large table. You hold a Magick Wand above your head with one hand. With the other hand, you point down at the objects on the table . . . . On the table is a Beautiful Lance, and a Silver Chalice, and a Shiny Sword, and a large, heavy coin, the size of a plate. Suddenly lightning strikes the tip of the Wand you are holding above your head. The lightning bolt flashes through your body and out the fingers of your other hand and onto the objects on the table. They now glow with magick light . . . . And so do you! In fact, YOU are that magick light.

Let's now be quiet for a moment and just observe what goes through your mind.

[Pause.]

If you need to write down a note, please do so now. Then close your eyes again.

[Pause.]

Now look again into the mirror while we chant. Again, imagine yourself kissing your Angel.

Path of Aleph

[WG blows E on the pitch pipe and leads the chant:]

Aahhhhhhh—Aahhhhhhh—Aahhhhhhh.

HT:
Finally, the color in the mirror changes to soft pale yellow. You can no longer see your reflection in the mirror . . . you smile as you realize that you . . . the *you* that you can no longer see . . . the *you* that has no reflection . . . exists on BOTH SIDES OF THE MIRROR at the same time. The idea pleases you. The idea actually makes you laugh like you've never laughed before. THERE IS NO YOU—YET—YOU ARE EVERYTHING AND NOTHING.

Now the mirror disappears into a BRILLIANT WHITE

. . . and you WAKE UP.

....

SLIDE # ?

Blank black.

....

HT:
You may now open your eyes.

And now, Friends and Comrades, we are done with our work for another season. Some, perhaps all of us, shall meet again someday. And some, perhaps none of us, shall ever meet again. Each of us is the star of our own adventure. For a moment in this dream of time, you have cast the Worthy Guide and myself and your fellow Comrades as characters in your movie. We thank you. It has truly been an honor. And, in return, I thank you all . . . for playing your roles so perfectly, and so exquisitely, in *my* movie.

[All retire for the night.]

O∴ H∴ O∴
THIRD-DEGREE
PORTFOLIO

FIGURE 15. THIRD-DEGREE STAR.

THIRD-DEGREE
STUDY PROGRAM

Nothing is too silly or frivolous if it provides the opportunity for you to familiarize yourself with the letters you are assigned to master.

Congratulations upon receiving your Third and final Degree Initiation. I sincerely hope that these ceremonial experiences have been both memorable and edifying for you, and that you feel enriched and transformed. The following material is intended to be suggestive of a course of study and practice to help you continue to digest, process, and synthesize the mysteries of the Third-Degree—and now, *all* three degrees.

As this is your third and final degree study program, you should also consider this your graduation assignments. Indeed, it *is* a graduation, and deserving of a few final words of Qabalistic encouragement. Please pay special attention to the "Valediction" at the conclusion of this study program.

Hebrew Letter & English	Name #	Full Spelling #	Meaning	Zodiac Sign & Tarot Trump	Color	Flashing Color	Music Note	Qabalistic Intelligence	Direction on Cube
ה HE	Heh 5	הה HH 10	Window	Aries & Emperor	Scarlet	Green	C	Constituting Intelligence	North-East edge
ו VW UO	Vav 6	וו VV 12	Nail	Taurus & Hierophant	Red Orange	Green Blue	C#	Triumphal Intelligence or Eternal Intelligence	South-East edge
ז Z	Zain 7	זין ZYN 67	Sword	Gemini & Lovers	Orange	Blue	D	Disposing Intelligence	East-Above edge
ח Ch H	Cheth 8	חית ChYTh 418	Fence Field	Cancer & Chariot	Amber	Indigo	D#	Intelligence of the House of Influence	East-Below edge
ט T	Teth 9	טית TYTh 419	Serpent	Leo & Strength	Yellow-Greenish	Crimson	E	Intelligence of all activities of the Spiritual Being	North-Above edge
י Y I J	Yod 10	יד YVD 20	Hand	Virgo & Hermit	Green-Yellowish	Deep Amber	F	Intelligence of Will	North-Below edge

TABLE 3. TABLE OF THE TWELVE SIMPLE LETTERS.

Hebrew Letter & English	Name #	Full Spelling #	Meaning	Zodiac Sign & Tarot Trump	Color	Flashing Color	Music Note	Qabalistic Intelligence	Direction on Cube
L (ל)	Lamed 30	למד LMD 74	Ox Goad	Libra & *Justice*	Emerald Green	Violet	F#	Faithful Intelligence	North-West Edge
N (נ)	Nun 50 or 700 Final ן	נון NVN 106	Fish	Scorpio & *Death*	Green-Blue	Reddish-Orange	G	Imaginative Intelligence	South-West edge
S (ס)	Samekh 60	סמך SMK 120	Tent Pole	Sagittarius & *Temperance*	Blue	Orange	G#	Intelligence of Probation or Tentative	West-Above edge
Au O U (ע)	Ayin 70	עין AYN 130	Eye	Capricorn & *Devil*	Indigo	Deep Amber	A	Renovating Intelligence	West-Below edge
Tz X (צ)	Tzaddi 90 or 900 Final ץ	צדי TzDY 104	Fish Hook	Aquarius & *Star*	Violet	Yellow	B♭	Natural Intelligence	South-Above edge
Q (ק)	Qoph 100	קוף QVP 186	Back of Head	Pisces & *Moon*	Crimson (ultra-violet)	Yellow Green	B	Corporeal Intelligence	South-Below edge

TABLE 3. TABLE OF THE TWELVE SIMPLE LETTERS.

PERPETUAL TINKERING

Now that all twenty-two letters have been psychically introduced and implanted in your psychic DNA, you may begin in earnest to "tinker" with the "Games Qabalists Play."[1] Pay special attention to the "Exercises and Meditations" section below.[2]

As always, be sure to review what was said in your First- and Second-Degree Portfolios about the Table of Letters and perpetually tinkering with the letters. You will again need to refer to other books in your own Qabalah reference library, without which your Qabalistic calculations will be impossible. For the Third-Degree, we especially recommend:

- *Sepher Yezirah*: in its entirety, especially Chapters V and VI. Also review as many different translations of the text as possible. Always keep in mind that many seemingly conflicting Qabalistic concepts can be simultaneously true; but to avoid being hopelessly confused, work only with one system at a time.

- *Chicken Qabalah*: Chapters III and X

- 777 and Other Qabalistic Writings

And for other topics of general research:

- Fractals. Look it up, and behold the Qabalistic wonders of fractals.

- The twelve signs of the zodiac; the twelve astrological houses; the zodiacal paths on the Tree of Life; and how the relationships of the elements and planets affect (and are affected *by*) each zodiac sign.

- Secondary colors of the rainbow, and the twelve-note musical scale.

In your journal, record your discoveries, revelations, or other Qabalistic synchronicities you observe.

INITIATION SCRIPT

It is your Great Work, as a Third-Degree Initiate, to deeply embed this ceremony in your psyche.

Please review what was said in your First- and Second-Degree Portfolios.

THIRD-DEGREE DODECAHEDRON TOY

Your primary Third-Degree toy is the *Dodecahedron* (twelve-sided solid) that figured so prominently in the *War of Roses* portion of your Third-Degree

Initiation ritual and lecture. While it was not immediately apparent to you, this twelve-sided solid is the perfect representation of all twenty-two letters of the Hebrew alphabet.

You will *play* with this toy as a meditation aid when attuning yourself to the Twelve Simple Letters, and when meditating on the infinitely changing relationships of all twenty-two letters. You are encouraged to create your own larger and more substantial version on heavy paper or card stock. Color it with the appropriate colors and add whatever other appropriate correspondences you discover in your studies. Seal within it your Second-Degree Cube, and within the cube, seal your First-Degree pipe cleaner toy.

Have fun with your toy. Create Qabalistic "games" to play with it. Generate words, numbers, and divinatory oracles by ceremonially "rolling the dice." Nothing is too silly or frivolous if it provides the opportunity for you to familiarize yourself with the letters you are assigned to master. Keep a record of the results of such games.

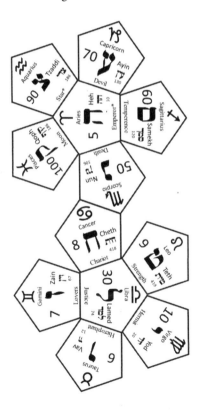

FIGURE 16. THIRD-DEGREE DODECAHEDRON TOY.

THIRD-DEGREE CUBE TOY

Your secondary Third-Degree toy is somewhat a consolation gift, because your Second-Degree Cube is now "officially" sealed within your Dodecahedron. You may or may not have noticed the Third-Degree Cube sitting on the table in the waiting area prior to your Third-Degree Initiation Ceremony. It is simply a version of your Second-Degree Cube with the addition of the Twelve Simple Letters and zodiac signs displayed along the edges.

Properly constructed, the Third-Degree Cube must include the First-Degree pipe cleaner star piercing through the top, bottom, and sides.

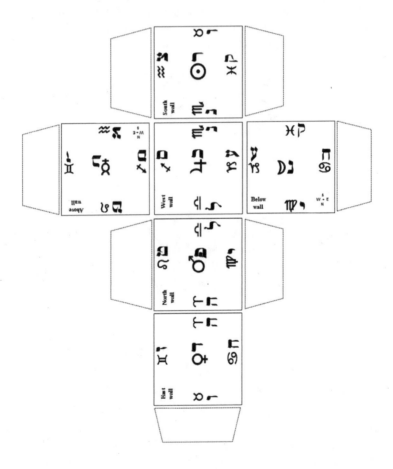

FIGURE 17. THIRD-DEGREE CUBE.

THIRD-DEGREE ART ASSIGNMENT #1

Construct a Simple Letter Dodecahedron Rattling Toy

You first art assignment is relatively simple. When it is completed, you will be rewarded with a handsome example of your rattling Third-Degree toy. You will again need a little help from a copy machine.

1. Make a copy of figure 17. (You can even enlarge it a bit if you like.) Print it on the heaviest white paper or card stock available to you.

2. Carefully cut out the pattern.

3. Fold at the lines. When you are done folding, your dodecahedron will almost form itself!

4. Tape each edge to its neighbor. (Some edges can be taped from the inside, but some, unfortunately, will need to be taped on the outside.)

   Note: To avoid this, before cutting out, you may wish to allow room for folding tabs along some of the edges, so they may be more easily taped on the inside, avoiding the necessity to leave exposed tape on the outside surface.

   Fold in such order that before you completely seal the dodecahedron, you can insert your Second-Degree Cube.

   Note: To make sure all twenty-two letters are included in your Dodecahedron Rattling Toy, be sure your Second-Degree Cube is properly pierced by your First-Degree pipe cleaner star.

For a more advanced project, you may wish to paint the dodecahedron and the letters with the appropriate colors and flashing colors.

THIRD-DEGREE ART ASSIGNMENT #2

Flash Card Color Images of the Twelve Simple Letters

Your second art assignment is to create twelve colored "flash cards" (one for each Simple letter) the same size and dimensions as those you created for the other letters. Do this by hand, not computer. When you have completed these, you will have a complete set of twenty-two colored flash cards.

You will find the appropriate colors itemized on the Table of Simple Letters.

For example, for Heh:

1. On a plain, *bright white* piece of 8½ × 11-inch heavy paper or card stock, lightly trace (in pencil) the outline of a large letter *Heh*.

2. Using *scarlet* oil, acrylic, or watercolor paint or pens, carefully fill in the Heh. Be careful to cover over or otherwise erase the pencil line.

   Make eleven more flash cards: one for Vav (red-orange); one for Zain (orange); one for Cheth (amber); one for Teth (yellow-greenish); one for Yod (green-yellowish); one for Lamed (emerald green); one for Nun (green-blue); one for Samekh (blue); one for Ayn (indigo); one for Tzaddi (Violet); and one for Qoph (crimson–ultraviolet).

   Also, as before, have an extra plain white sheet that will be used in the exercise.

And, as you are working on your art projects: Remember what was said to you in your First- and Second-Degree Portfolios about colors, fragrances, and sense associations, while working with projects associated with the individual letters.

Your Third-Degree Home Temple and Altar

As a Third-Degree Initiate, you are now not only Master of the Twelve Simple Letters, you are Master of the entire Hebrew alphabet. Your First-Degree Temple and Altar were constructed and adorned with those things associated with the Mother Letters; your Second-Degree Temple and Altar with those of the Double Letters. Obviously, the accoutrements of your Third-Degree Temple should incorporate things associated with the Simple Letters—but more than that—your Third-Degree Temple should (with *Balance, Harmony,* and *Beauty*) perfectly synthesize the essence of *all the letters.*

Your Altar should be illuminated by the three candles of the First-Degree candelabra *and* the seven candles of the Second-Degree Menorah. Other than this suggestion, it is entirely up to you (as a Qabalah artist) how best to arrange and adorn your Temple. You're a Qabalah grownup now! From this point on, all your formal Qabalah work—your practices, exercises, meditations, prayers, magic, and journaling—will be done in this Third-Degree Temple. It is your natural habitat.

Exercises and Meditations

These are a few exercises, meditations, and practices recommended for you as a Third-Degree Initiate. As with the exercises of the previous degrees, they are designed to attune you to the specific agencies and powers of consciousness associated with the degree (in this case, the Twelve Simple Letters of the Hebrew alphabet). As always, these exercises are not difficult and do not require a great deal of time to execute. It is hoped that you will continue with your daily routine and diligently follow it for at least a period of *ninety days,* and after that, whenever you feel the need to re-attune yourself.

These exercises should, of course, be accompanied and enhanced (whenever possible and practical) by the appropriate incense or scents, music, and temple colors associated in your mind with the specific letter or letters being worked.

Once you have mastered these preliminary exercises, you are encouraged to design rituals and practices of your own, based upon your increasing mastery of the mysteries of the Twelve Simple Letters.

∴

SIMPLE THIRD-DEGREE
HOME TEMPLE OPENING

*[To be performed prior to other home
rituals, exercises, or meditations.]*

*[On the altar are placed both the
candelabra and Menorah—unlit.]*

[Sit comfortably before the Altar and clap twelve times 4-4-4.]

*[Strike a match and light the black Tav candle
and pluck it from the Menorah.]*

The Point said, "I AM."

*[Using the flame of Tav, light the Aleph, Mem,
and Shin candles of the candelabra.]*

The Point burst as three extended rays.

*[Replace the Tav candle to the center of the
Menorah and pluck the Aleph candle.]*

*[Using the Aleph candle, light the Beth and
Gimel candles of the Menorah.]*

[Replace the Aleph candle and pluck the Mem candle.]

*[Using the Mem candle, light the Daleth
and Kaph candles of the Menorah.]*

[Replace the Mem candle and pluck the Shin candle.]

*[Using the Shin candle, light the Peh and
Resh candles of the Menorah.]*

The Three Rays sealed the limits of space and time . . .

[Replace the Shin candle in the Menorah.]

. . . and provoked a twelvefold War of Roses.

[Clap twelve times 4-4-4.]

The Temple is open.

∴

AMSH WARM-UP EXERCISE
[from First-Degree is still recommended.]

∴

DAWN AMSH BREATH CYCLE
[from First-Degree is still recommended.]

∴

PASSING THE PYLONS
Astral Projection into the World of the Simple Letters

As with the other letters, the purpose of the exercise is to attune and acclimate your psychic body to the particular frequency of consciousness
(Qabalistic Intelligence) exemplified by each Simple Letter (see the description in the Third-Degree Portfolio) by projecting one's consciousness
through the color-polarized floating "ghost image" of the letter, by means of
the technique employed in the initiation ceremonies.

Materials Needed:

- Pitch pipe
- Flash cards of Twelve Letters
  - Scarlet *Heh*
  - Red-orange *Vav*
  - Orange *Zain*
  - Amber *Cheth*
  - Yellow-greenish *Teth*
  - Green-yellowish *Yod*
  - Emerald-green *Lamed*
  - Green-blue *Nun*
  - Blue *Samekh*
  - Indigo *Ayin*
  - Violet *Tzaddi*
  - Crimson (ultraviolet) *Qoph*
- Blank white card
- Bright light

∴

PASSING THE PYLONS
Skrying Exercise

Example: Heh

1. Carefully mount your blank white flash card at the *center right* of your Altar; and directly beside it (at the *center left* of the Altar), mount your scarlet Heh flash card.

2. Shine a bright light in such a way that it vibrantly illuminates both cards but does not shine into your eyes.

3. Comfortably seat yourself as near as possible to the two cards so that when you gaze at the letter, it essentially fills your field of vision.

4. Take your pitch pipe, find the C note, and blow.

5. Take a deep breath and forcefully sing, "Hahhhhhhh." *(Repeat three times.)*

6. Relax and gaze at the brightly illuminated scarlet Heh. Keep staring at the letter until it starts to do strange things.

7. Then quickly turn your gaze to the plain white blank card.

   a. You should see a *green* Heh floating over the white card. That ghost image is your gateway—your pylon.

   b. If you close your eyes and wait for a moment, the green ghost Heh will clearly appear on the screen of your inner eyelids and remain floating for several seconds. If this doesn't happen, repeat steps 6 and 7 until it does.

8. When you have mastered the art of creating the ghost image of the letter on the screen of your closed eyes, you'll be ready to project your consciousness through the pylon and enter in vision the "world" of the letter.

9. The moment the ghost image is firmly visible on your closed eyes, make the First-Degree Sign[3] and whisper, "Ahhhhhhh-Mmmmmmmmm-Shhhhhhh." Imagine yourself passing through the green letter Heh as if it were a letter-shaped puff of smoke.

10. Now, just relax and begin your skrying session.

11. When you sense you have "seen" enough for this session, use your imagination to pass back into your Temple by again giving the First-Degree Sign and Word. Then open your eyes and clap twelve times.

12. Important: Immediately write down in your journal the details of *everything* you saw or everything you thought about during the skrying session. Don't omit anything, no matter how insignificant you might think it is. You will analyze it later.

The procedure for the eleven other Simple Letters (Vav, Zain, Cheth, Teth, Yod, Lamed, Nun, Samekh, Ayin, Tzaddi, and Qoph) is exactly as in the Heh example, but with appropriate changes to colors, musical notes, and words vibrated.

Heh

Image on card:	Scarlet Heh
Pitch pipe note:	C
Word sung:	Hahhhhhhh
Ghost Heh:	Green

Vav

Image on card:	Red-Orange Vav
Pitch pipe note:	C#
Word sung:	Vahhhhhhh
Ghost Vav:	Green Blue

Zain

Image on card:	Orange Zain
Pitch pipe note:	D
Word sung:	Zahhhhhhh
Ghost Zain:	Blue

Cheth

Image on card:	Amber Cheth
Pitch pipe note:	D#
Word sung:	Hcahhhhhhh
Ghost Cheth:	Indigo

Teth

Image on card:	Yellow-Greenish Teth
Pitch pipe note:	E
Word sung:	Tahhhhhhh
Ghost Teth:	Crimson

Yod

Image on card:	Green-Yellowish Yod
Pitch pipe note:	F
Word sung:	Yahhhhhhh
Ghost Yod:	Deep Amber

Lamed

Image on card:	Emerald-Green Lamed
Pitch pipe note:	F#
Word sung:	Lahhhhhhh
Ghost Lamed:	Violet

Nun

Image on card:	Green-Blue Nun
Pitch pipe note:	G
Word sung:	Nahhhhhhh
Ghost Nun:	Reddish Orange

Samekh

Image on card:	Blue Samekh
Pitch pipe note:	G#
Word sung:	Sahhhhhhh
Ghost Samekh:	Orange

Ayin

Image on card:	Indigo Ayin
Pitch pipe note:	A
Word sung:	Oyahhhhhhh
Ghost Ayin:	Deep Amber

Tzaddi

Image on card:	Violet Tzaddi
Pitch pipe note:	B$^\flat$
Word sung:	Tzahhhhhhh
Ghost Tzaddi:	Yellow

Qoph

Image on card:	Crimson (ultraviolet) Qoph
Pitch pipe note:	B
Word sung	Qahhhhhhh
Ghost Qoph:	Yellow Green

∴

AUGURY AND DIVINATION
Daily Oracle Exercise

It is a well-known fact that the Hebrew alphabet has a direct correlation to the twenty-two Tarot card trumps. But Tarot is not the only way the sacred alphabet can be utilized for divinatory purposes. Now that you are armed with all twenty-two letters of the Hebrew alphabet, you can perform all manner of divinatory exercises, selecting a small number of randomly generated letters for the purpose of general augury or to answer specific questions.

Possible techniques and applications are limited only by your own imagination. I suggest that you start your exploration by seeking a generic "daily oracle" from three randomly generated Hebrew letters. The technique is simple, but the insights about yourself that you can gain can be profound and life changing.

1. Randomly generate three Hebrew letters. (If you have a twenty-two-sided gaming die, you could simply roll it three times; or any way you can devise to arrive at three numbers between 1 and 22.)

2. Write down all the permutations (*i.e.*, ABC, BCA, CAB, CBA, ACB, BAC).

   a. Using your Hebrew/English Dictionary, determine what, if anything, these letters actually spell in Hebrew. (They might even spell something in English!)

   b. Using your 777 Tables, explore other Qabalistic words of significance that share the same number.

   c. Continue to tinker with the letters using every technique of "games Qabalists play."

   d. Even if you do not understand the "oracle," record the results and your impressions in your journal.

VALEDICTION

As I've repeatedly reminded you, Qabalah is a system of organizing your mind so that it may more perfectly reflect the Universal Consciousness of Existence itself, and Qabalistic exercises and meditations are designed to show us how everything in our world is connected to everything else, how everything is the reflection of everything else, and how every idea and thought are connected to every other idea and thought. Modern mathematics offers us a perfectly beautiful and elegant model of what Qabalists (kabbalists/cabalists) have been working with for centuries: fractals.

Fractals are a mathematical phenomenon that occurs on all levels of nature. Expressed graphically, fractals generate similar replicating patterns at increasingly larger and/or increasingly smaller scales—each level almost identical to the level above it and to the level below it ("evolving" or "expanding symmetry"). You've probably seen artistically stunning computer-generated examples of fractals. The natural laws that are illustrated by fractals are also on display at all times in terms of *consciousness.*

The Supreme Consciousness of Godhead is the master pattern; and the infinite multiplicity of all facets of manifest creation (including you and me, and the dimension and objective "reality" we believe we inhabit) is merely a *fractal chain reaction* of God-consciousness. *Consciousness.* The primary Hermetic axiom "As above, so below" and the Qabalistic adage "Kether is in Malkuth, and Malkuth is in Kether, only after another manner" are explicit declarations of this fundamental truth.

The alphanumeric properties of the twenty-two letters of the Hebrew alphabet are the building blocks of the fractal patterns of consciousness. That is why the classic Qabalah-based "God Names" and the traditional names of archangels, angels, intelligences, and spirits are often found to be mathematically linked to each other by prime numbers or other numeric harmonics based on the number of a specific Sephirah or Path.

For example, some of the "angels" traditionally associated with the Planetary Sphere of Mercury (Sephirah #8) are the Intelligence,

"Tirial":

(לאיריט)

([Heb: reading right to left, Teth, Yod, Resh, Yod, Aleph, Lamed])

$(לאיריט) = 260 = \Sigma\{1 - (8 \times 8)\} \div 8$

and the Spirit,

"Taphthartharath":

(תרתרתפת)

([Heb: reading right to left, Tav, Peh, Tav, Resh, Tav, Resh, Tav])

$\left(תרתרתפת\right)$ = 2080 = $\Sigma\{1 - (64$ or $8^2)$.

Also, two Intelligences traditionally associated with the zodiac sign Gemini (which is ruled by Mercury) are

"Din":

(דין)

([Heb: reading right to left, Daleth, Yod, Nun])

$\left(דין\right)$ = 64 or 8^2

and

"Doni":

(ינד)

([Heb: reading right to left, Daleth, Nun, Yod])

$\left(ינד\right)$ = 64 or 8^2

Obviously, the number eight (and all cosmic and abstract meanings to all things eight-ish) is the common denomination and "tonic" note within which these "spirits" vibrate and harmonize at their specific level. But as you thumb through all the reference books in your library, you will encounter hundreds of examples where these alphanumeric harmonies *do not* neatly appear in a consistent manner. That is to be expected, given the fact that most of our reference books are compilations from multiple sources written and rewritten, translated and retranslated from Hebrew to multiple languages, all with different pronunciations and renderings of Hebrew—some even mixed with Greek and Latin and then into English!

However, it is abundantly clear that in the mythical "Eden" of the ideal and pristine Qabalah, the divine letters began as the perfect alphanumeric building blocks forming divine *words*, which were the perfect alphanumeric building blocks forming divine *sentences*, which were the perfect alphanumeric building blocks forming divine *paragraphs*, which were the perfect alphanumeric building blocks forming divine *chapters*, which were the perfect alphanumeric building blocks of the *Book of Life* itself . . . to the *Mind of God* itself.

Tiriel, and Taphthartharath, and Din and Doni may hold a special place in your tradition-loving heart, and indeed you might want to consciously "work" with them as Mercurial forces or in raising your consciousness to the level of Sephirah Hod, or to the Path of Zain on the Tree of Life. But Tiriel, and Taphthartharath, and Din and Doni (and all the traditional angels and spirits of the Qabalah and medieval magick) are not in and of themselves crystalized or sacrosanct magical "beings" living objective lives in some Qabalistic boarding house.

Hell, no! Some real-live person in the past made them up! Somebody just like you used their Qabalah skills and imagination and invented all the gods, the archangels, angels, *intelligences, spirits, and demons.*

As a matter of fact, using your mastery of the Hebrew alphabet, *you* could (right now) set to work to create your own personal and unique eight-based pantheon of spiritual forces all your own. You could build their names from Hebrew letters enumerating to numbers that have eight as a conspicuous factor. Your knowledge of the proper colors reveals what these angels look like; your knowledge of their elemental, planetary, or zodiacal makeup reveals their specific powers and gifts.

Think about it—your own private hierarchy of spiritual beings—immediately and intimately linked to you, because they are *your* creations. That's the kind of thing grown-up Qabalists do! That's what Qabalah is about!

And now, my dear Friend and Comrade, here at the conclusion of your initiatory journey, I am suggesting that you do just that! Create your own angels! Create your own personal *Hierarchy of Heaven.* Think of it as an exercise, or think of it as your Great Work!

Make it simple:

- God Name
- Archangel (who works for God Name)
- Angel (who works for Archangel)
- Intelligence (who works for Angel)
- Spirit (who works for Intelligence)

Start out with the Tree of Life as your ladder, reaching up through levels of consciousness: Base your first set of names on number Ten, then Nine, then Eight, then Seven, Six, Five, Four, Three, Two, and finally One (that'll be a challenge).

You don't think you can do something like this?

HELL, YES! You can do it! You're a Chicken Qabalist!

Don't Worry About It!

Just Start!

EPILOGUE

By Lon Milo DuQuette

Instruction is found in the noise of speech. But the Wisdom of the Holy Teachings is heard only in the Silence. . . . Forms and shapes and colors hide the Soul of Creation. But the Beauty of the Holy Teachings is seen equally in the Darkness and the Light.

—Rabbi Lamed Ben Clifford
from the First-Degree Initiation

It is often said that an artist never finishes a creation but simply abandons it. It certainly feels that way to me. Over the last thirty years I have written quite a number of books, songs, articles, and essays, and, I confess (with no small measure of frustration), they all remain abandoned *works-in-progress.* The present book has proved to be no exception.

Nonetheless, I believe this is how it always must be if my work is truly a "creation." After all, parents lovingly shelter, nourish, and instruct their children (indeed, many parents persist forever). But, naturally, there comes a time when the child, as a viable creature, must be unleashed upon the universe to do whatever must be done in order to fulfill and exhaust his or her cosmic potentiality. And so, I am about to abandon another child and unleash it upon the world to (for good or ill) exhaust its cosmic potentiality.

It has been my honor and my pleasure to serve as biographer, curator, and editor on behalf of Rabbi Lamed Ben Clifford. His adolescent impatience with petrified traditions (and his insistence that any spiritual study is useless, unless it facilitates some degree of self-transformation and illumination) mirrors uncannily my own.

I'm sure there will be those who will be disappointed that this book does not shed new light on the elegant minutia of the *Torah* or *Sepher Yetzirah* or *Heichalot* or *Bahir* or *Zohar* or *Sefer Raziel HaMalakh,* or *Liber AL vel Legis,* or spend time playing Gematria games or stacking *Qliphoth* under *Intelligences* under *Angels* under *Archangels* under *God Names.* But frankly, those debates (from highly knowledgeable participants) can be found in abundance with a single click on a computer link.

The rabbi made it clear in the First-Degree Lecture that such Qabalistic tinkerings will always play a part in every Qabalist's personal work and recreation, and the reference material for such exercises is easily found. But he also cautioned that enmeshing the mind (Ruach) in this stuff before the Soul (Neshamah) is prepared is like

> casting the seeds of the Hebrew alphabet upon the surface of untilled land. They'll *sit* there—in their unique beauty and potentiality. But, unless the earth is first broken and plowed, the seeds will never take root and grow. They will just remain on the surface as husks—rattling noisily against one another in the wind.[1]

I hope the reader will at least try to appreciate what the rabbi was attempting to do with the initiation ceremonies, toys, exercises, and meditations of "Our Holy Order." Hopefully, I have organized the material in such a way that your reading experience has itself been an initiatory experience, and that the seeds of the Hebrew alphabet are now stirring and sprouting in your newly mutated Neshamah.

For those of you who may wish to actually dramatically stage these ceremonies for the purpose of initiating others (a little *Our Holy Order* of your own), I'm sure the rabbi would be pleased and gratified. However, if that is truly your intent, I urge you to always honor his vision of a free, nonhierarchical, and classless band of Qabalah Friends and Comrades *who meet and work only when and where your dreams intersect.*

APPENDIX I

CHICKEN QABALIST'S REFERENCE LIBRARY[1]

Ben Yehuda. *Hebrew/English Dictionary*. Pocket Books, 1989.

Buschoff, Dr. Erich. *The Kabbalah*. Most recent reprint, York Beach, ME: Samuel Weiser, Inc., 1985.

Crowley, Aleister. *The Book of Thoth: A Short Essay on the Tarot of the Egyptians*. The Master Therion. London: O.T.O., 1944.

_____. *The Equinox* III (5). Facsimile edition. York Beach, ME: Samuel Weiser, 1991.

_____. *The Qabalah of Aleister Crowley*. New York: Samuel Weiser, 1973. Retitled *777 and Other Qabalistic Writings of Aleister Crowley* in the fifth printing, 1977. Reprinted York Beach, ME: Samuel Weiser, 1990.

DuQuette, Lon Milo. *Angels, Demons & Gods of the New Millennium*. York Beach, ME: Samuel Weiser, 1997.

_____. *The Chicken Qabalah of Rabbi Lamed Ben Clifford*. York Beach, ME: Samuel Weiser, 2001.

_____. *Tarot of Ceremonial Magick*. York Beach, ME: Samuel Weiser, 1993.

_____. *Understanding Aleister Crowley's Thoth Tarot*. York Beach, ME: Weiser Books, 2003.

Fortune, Dion. *The Mystical Qabalah*. London: Ernest Benn Limited, 1976.

Friedman, Irving. *The Book of Creation*. York Beach, ME: Samuel Weiser, Inc., 1977.

Godwin, David. *Godwin's Cabalistic Encyclopedia*. Minneapolis, MN: Llewellyn Publications, 2017.

Kalisch, Isidor. *Sepher Yezirah: A Book on Creation, or the Jewish Metaphysics of Remote Antiquity*. New York: L. H. Frank & Co., 1877. Rosicrucian Order AMORC, 15th edition, San Jose, CA: 2002.

Kaplan, Aryeh. tr. *The Bahir*. York Beach, ME: Samuel Weiser, 1990.

_____. *Sepher Yetzerah*. York Beach, ME: Samuel Weiser, 1990.

Lamsa, George M. tr. *The Holy Bible*. Philadelphia: A. J. Holman Company, 1967.

Levi, Eliphas. *The Key of the Mysteries*. Tr. Aleister Crowley. New York: Samuel Weiser, 1973.

Mathers, S. L. ed. and tr. *The Kabbalah Unveiled*. London: Kegan Paul, Trench and Trubner, 1887; reprinted York Beach, ME: Samuel Weiser, 1993.

Mordell, Phineas. *The Origin of Letters and Numerals According to the Sefer Yetzirah*. York Beach, ME: Samuel Weiser, Inc., 1975.

Munk, Michael L. *The Wisdom in the Hebrew Alphabet*. Brooklyn, NY: Mesorah Publications, LTD, 1983.

Ponce, Charles. *Kabbalah: An Introduction and Illumination for the World Today*. San Francisco: Quest Books, 1978.

Roth, Cecil. *Encyclopedia Judaica*. New York: MacMillan Co., 1972.

Scholem, Gershom. ed. *Zohar, The Book of Splendor: Basic Readings from the Kabbalah*. New York: Schocken Books, Inc., 1972.

Singer, Isidore. *The Jewish Encyclopedia*. New York: Ktav Publishing, 1964.

Skinner, Stephen. *The Complete Magician's Tables*. Minneapolis, MN: Llewellyn Publications, 2007.

Sternring, Knut. *The Book of Formation*. New York: Ktav Publishing, 1970.

Suares, Carlo. *The Sepher Yetsira*. Tr. Micheline & Vincent Stuart. Boulder, CO and London: Shambhala, 1976.

Townley, Kevin. *The Cube of Space, Container of Creation*. Boulder, CO: Archive Press, 1993.

Waite, Arthur Edward. *The Holy Kabbalah*. New York: University Books, 1972.

Wang, Robert. *Qabalistic Tarot*. York Beach, ME: Samuel Weiser, Inc., 1990.

Westcott, W. Wynn. *Sepher Yetzirah: The Book of Formation and the Thirty-Two Paths of Wisdom*. York Beach, ME: Samuel Weiser, Inc., 1975.

APPENDIX II

THE THIRTY-TWO
PATHS OF WISDOM[1]

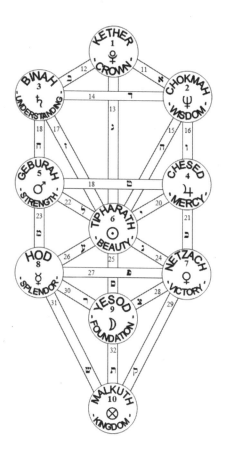

FIGURE 18.

The **First Path** is called the *Admirable* or the *Hidden Intelligence* (the Highest Crown), for it is the Light giving the power of comprehension of that First Principle, which has no beginning; and it is the Primal Glory, for no created being can attain to its essence.

The **Second** Path is that of the *Illuminating Intelligence*; it is the Crown of Creation, the Splendor of the Unity, equaling it, and it is exalted above every head, and named by the Kabbalists the Second Glory.

The **Third Path** is the *Sanctifying Intelligence* and is the basis of foundation of Primordial Wisdom, which is called the Former of Faith, and its roots, Amen; and it is the parent of Faith, from whose virtues doth Faith emanate.

The **Fourth Path** is named *Measuring, Cohesive* or *Receptacular*; and so because it contains all the holy powers, and from it emanate all the spiritual virtues with the most exalted essences, they emanate one from the other by the power of the primordial emanation.

The **Fifth Path** is called the *Radical Intelligence*, because it is itself the essence equal to the Unity, uniting itself to the Binah, or Intelligence, which emanates from the primordial depths of Wisdom or Chokmah.

The **Sixth Path** is called the *Intelligence of the Mediating Influence*, because in it are multiplied the influxes of the emanations, for it causes that influence to flow into all the reservoirs of the Blessings, with which these themselves are united.

The **Seventh Path** is the *Occult Intelligence*, because it is the Refulgent Splendor of all the Intellectual virtues, which are perceived by the eyes of intellect and by the contemplation of faith.

The **Eighth Path** is called *Absolute or Perfect*, because it is the means of the primordial, which has no root by which it can cleave, nor rest, except in the hidden places of Gedulah (*Chesed*), Magnificence, which emanate from its own proper essence.

The **Ninth Path** is the *Pure Intelligence*, so called because it purifies the Numerations; it proves and corrects the designing of their representation and disposes their unity with which they are combined without diminution or division.

The **Tenth Path** is the *Resplendent Intelligence*, because it is exalted above every head and sits on the throne of Binah (the Intelligence spoken of in the Third Path). It illuminates the splendor of all the lights and causes a supply of influence to emanate from the Prince of countenances.

The **Eleventh Path** is the *Scintillating Intelligence*, because it is the essence of that curtain which is placed close to the order of the disposition, and this is a special dignity given to it that it may be able to stand before the Face of the Cause of Causes.

The **Twelfth Path** is the *Intelligence of Transparency* because it is that species of Magnificence called Chazchazit, which is named the place whence issues the vision of those seeing in apparitions. (That is, the prophecies by seers in a vision.)

The **Thirteenth Path** is named the *Uniting Intelligence*, and it is so called because it is itself the Essence of Glory. It is the Consummation of the Truth of individual spiritual things.

The **Fourteenth Path** is the *Illuminating Intelligence* and is so called because it is that Brilliant One that is the founder of the concealed and fundamental ideas of holiness and of their stages of preparation.

The **Fifteenth Path** is the *Constituting Intelligence*, so called because it constitutes the substance of creation in pure darkness, and men have spoken of these contemplations; it is that darkness spoken of in Scripture, Job xxxviii. 9, "and thick darkness a swaddling band for it."

The **Sixteenth Path** is the *Triumphal* or *Eternal Intelligence*, so called because it is the pleasure of the Glory, beyond which is no other Glory like to it, and it is called also the Paradise prepared for the Righteous.

The **Seventeenth Path** is the *Disposing Intelligence*, which provides Faith to the Righteous, and they are clothed with the Holy Spirit by it, and it is called the Foundation of Excellence in the state of higher things.

The **Eighteenth Path** is called the *House of Influence* (by the greatness of whose abundance the influx of good things upon created beings is increased), and from the midst of investigation the arcana and hidden senses are drawn forth, which dwell in its shade and which cling to it, from the cause of all causes.

The **Nineteenth Path** is the *Intelligence of All the Activities of the Spiritual Beings* and is so called because of the affluence diffused by it from the most-high blessing and most exalted sublime glory.

The **Twentieth Path** is the *Intelligence of Will* and is so called because it is the means of preparation of all and each created being, and by this intelligence the existence of the Primordial Wisdom becomes known.

The **Twenty-first Path** is the *Intelligence of Conciliation* and is so called because it receives the divine influence that flows into it from its benediction upon all and each existence.

The **Twenty-second Path** is the *Faithful Intelligence* and is so called because by it spiritual virtues are increased, and all dwellers on earth are nearly under its shadow.

The **Twenty-third Path** is the *Stable Intelligence*, and it is so called because it has the virtue of consistency among all numerations.

The **Twenty-fourth Path** is the *Imaginative Intelligence*, and it is so called because it gives a likeness to all the similitudes, which are created in like manner similar to its harmonious elegancies.

The **Twenty-fifth Path** is the *Intelligence of Probation*, or is *Tentative*, and is so called because it is the primary temptation by which the Creator trieth all righteous persons.

The **Twenty-sixth Path** is called the *Renovating Intelligence*, because the Holy God renews by it all the changing things that are renewed by the creation of the world.

The **Twenty-seventh Path** is the *Active* or *Exciting Intelligence* and is so called because through it every existent being receives its spirit and motion.

The **Twenty-eighth Path** is called the *Natural Intelligence* and is so called because through it is consummated and perfected the nature of every existent being under the orb of the sun, in perfection.

The **Twenty-ninth Path** is the *Corporeal Intelligence*, so called because it forms every body that is formed beneath the whole set of worlds and the increment of them.

The **Thirtieth Path** is the *Collecting Intelligence* and is so called because astrologers deduce from it the judgment of the stars, and the celestial signs, and the perfections of their science, according to the rules of their revolutions.

The **Thirty-first Path** is the *Perpetual Intelligence*; but why is it so called? Because it regulates the motions of the Sun and Moon in their proper order, each in an orbit convenient for it.

The **Thirty-second Path** is the *Administrative Intelligence*, and it is so called because it directs and associates in all their operations the seven planets, even all of them in their own due courses.

THIRTY-TWO MYSTERIOUS PATHS OF WISDOM

Path 1

Kether

Admirable Intelligence or Concealed Intelligence

(The Highest Crown)

It is the Light giving the power of comprehension of that First Principle, which has no beginning. It is the Primal Glory, for no created being can attain to its essence.

Path 2

Chokmah

Illuminating Intelligence

(The Second Glory)

It is the Crown of Creation, and the Splendor of the Unity, equaling it.

It is exalted above every head (Sephirah).

Path 3

Binah

Sanctifying Intelligence

The basis of foundation of Primordial Wisdom, which is called the *Former of Faith*, and its roots.

It is the parent of Faith, from which virtues Faith emanates.

Path 4

Chesed

Measuring, Cohesive, or Receptacular Intelligence

It is so called because it contains all the holy powers, and from it emanate all the spiritual virtues with the most exalted essences; they emanate one from the other by the power of the primordial emanation (The Highest Crown).

Path 5

Geburah

Radical Intelligence

It is so called because it is itself the essence equal to the Unity, uniting itself to the Binah, or Intelligence, which emanates from the primordial depths of Wisdom or Chokmah.

Path 6

Tiphareth

Intelligence of the Mediating Influence

In it are multiplied the influxes of the emanations, for it causes that influence to flow into all the reservoirs of the Blessings, with which these themselves are united.

Path 7

Netzach

Occult (Hidden) Intelligence

It is the *Refulgent Splendor* of all the Intellectual virtues, which are perceived by the eyes of intellect and by the contemplation of faith.

Path 8

Hod

Absolute or Perfect Intelligence

It is the means of the primordial, which has no root by which it can cleave, nor rest, except in the hidden places of Gedulah, Magnificence, which emanate from its own proper essence.

Path 9

Yesod

Pure Intelligence

It purifies the Numerations.

It proves and corrects the designing of their representation and disposes of their unity with which they are combined without diminution or division.

Path 10

Malkuth

The Resplendent Intelligence

It is exalted above every head, and sits on the throne of Binah (the Intelligence spoken of in the Third Path).

It illuminates the splendor of all lights and causes a supply of influence to emanate from the Prince of countenances.

Path 11

Aleph—Fool

Path 1 to 2

Scintillating Intelligence

It is the essence of that curtain that is placed close to the order of the disposition, and this is a special dignity given to it that it may be able to stand before the Face of the Cause of Causes.

Path 12

Beth—Magician

Path 1 to 3

Intelligence of Transparency

It is that species of Magnificence called Chazchazit, which is named the place whence issues the vision of those seeing in apparitions. (That is, the prophecies by seers in a vision.)

Path 13

Gimel—High Priestess

Path 1 to 6

Uniting Intelligence

The Uniting Intelligence is so called because it is itself the essence of Glory. It is the Consummation of the Truth of individual spiritual things.

Path 14

Daleth—Empress

Path 2 to 3

Illuminating Intelligence

Illuminating Intelligence is so called because it is itself that Chashmal that is the founder of the concealed and fundamental ideas of holiness and of their stages of preparation.

Path 15

Heh—Emperor (*Star)

Path 2 to 6

Constituting Intelligence

Constituting Intelligence is so called because it constitutes the substance of creation in pure darkness, and men have spoken of these contemplations; it is that darkness spoken of in scripture, Job xxxviii. 9, "and thick darkness a swaddling band for it."

Path 16

Vav—Hierophant

Path 2 to 4

Triumphal Intelligence

(Eternal One)

Triumphal or Eternal Intelligence is so called because it is the pleasure of the Glory, beyond which is no other Glory like to it, and it is called also the Paradise prepared for the Righteous.

Path 17

Zain—Lovers

Path 3 to 6

Disposing One

The Disposing Intelligence provides Faith to the Righteous, and they are clothed with the Holy Spirit by it, and it is called the *Foundation of Excellence* in the state of higher things.

Path 18

Cheth—Chariot

Path 3 to 5

Intelligence of the House of Influence

The House of Influence (by the greatness of whose abundance the influx of good things upon created beings is increased): from the midst of the investigation the arcana and hidden senses are drawn forth, which dwell in its shade and which cling to it, from the cause of all causes.

Path 19

Teth—Strength

Path 4 to 5

Intelligence of All the Activities of the Spiritual Beings

The Nineteenth Path is the Intelligence of All the Activities of the Spiritual Beings and is so called because of the affluence diffused by it from the most high blessing and most exalted sublime glory.

Path 20

Yod—Hermit

Path 4 to 6

Intelligence of Will

The Intelligence of Will, is so called because it is the means of preparation of all and each created being, and by this intelligence the existence of the Primordial Wisdom becomes known.

Path 21

Kaph—Wheel of Fortune

Path 4 to 7

Intelligence of Conciliation

The Intelligence of Conciliation is so called because it receives the divine influence that flows into it from its benediction upon all and each existence.

Path 22

Lamed—Justice

Path 5 to 6

Faithful Intelligence

The Faithful Intelligence is so called because by it spiritual virtues are increased, and all dwellers on earth are nearly under its shadow.

Path 23

Mem—Hanged Man

Path 5 to 8

Stable Intelligence

The Stable Intelligence is so called because it has the virtue of consistency among all numerations.

(Multiply any number by 9 and the resulting number will always reduce to 9; e.g., 9 × 3 = 27; 2 + 7 = 9.)

Path 24

Nun—Death

Path 6 to 7

Imaginative Intelligence

The Imaginative Intelligence is so called because it gives a likeness to all the similitudes, which are created in like manner similar to its harmonious elegancies.

Path 25

Samekh–Temperance

Path 6 to 9

Intelligence of Probation

The Intelligence of Probation (or *Tentative*) is so called because it is the primary temptation by which the Creator (blessed be He) tests all righteous persons.

Path 26

Ayin—Devil

Path 6 to 8

Renovating Intelligence

The Twenty-sixth Path is called the Renovating Intelligence, because the Holy God (blessed be He) renews by it all the changing things that are renewed by the creation of the world.

Path 27

Peh—Tower

Path 7 to 8

Exciting Intelligence

The Twenty-seventh Path is the Exciting Intelligence, and it is so called because by it is created the Intellect of all created beings under the highest heaven, and the excitement or motion of them.

Path 28

Tzaddi—Star (*Emperor)

Path 7 to 9

Natural Intelligence

The Natural Intelligence is so called because through it is consummated and perfected the nature of every existent being under the orb of the sun, in perfection.

Path 29

Qoph—Moon

Path 7 to 10

Corporeal Intelligence

The Corporeal Intelligence is so called because it forms every body that is formed beneath the whole set of worlds and the increment of them.

Path 30

Resh—Sun

Path 8 to 9

Collecting Intelligence

The Collecting Intelligence is so called because astrologers deduce from it the judgment of the stars, and of the celestial signs, and the perfections of their science, according to the rules of their revolutions.

Path 31

Shin—Judgment (*Aeon)

Path 7 to 10

Perpetual Intelligence

The Perpetual Intelligence is so called because it regulates the motions of the Sun and Moon in their proper order, each in an orbit convenient for it.

Path 32

Vav—Universe

Path 9 to 10

Administrative Intelligence

The Administrative Intelligence is so called because it directs and associates in all their operations the seven planets, even all of them in their own due courses.

Group Exercise

Form together in groups of three or two.

Each member randomly selects a Path (from 11–32).

Discuss *WHY* you think your particular "Intelligence" is appropriate to link the two Sephiroth that your path connects.

ENDNOTES

Author's Notes

1   *Yetzirah* is sometimes spelled *Yezirah*.

2   The rabbi seemed happy with the adjustments made by the adepts of the Hermetic Order of the Golden Dawn at the end of the nineteenth century. He penciled in their adjustments to the text of his own preferred translation by Isidor Kalisch: *Sepher Yezirah: A Book on Creation, or the Jewish Metaphysics of Remote Antiquity* (New York: L. H. Frank & Co., 1877). New editions have been published by the Rosicrucian Order AMORC, 15th edition (San Jose, CA: 2002).

3   *The Qabalah of Aleister Crowley* (New York: Samuel Weiser, 1973). Retitled *777 and Other Qabalistic Writings of Aleister Crowley,* in the fifth printing, 1977 (reprinted York Beach, ME: Samuel Weiser, 1990).

4   It was rumored Ben Clifford had been involved with the celebrated San Francisco gossip columnist and hostess, albeit in the milieu of their previous incarnations in ancient Atlantis.

Prologue

1   Gershom G. Scholem, *Zohar: The Book of Splendor: Basic Readings from the Kabbalah* (New York: Schocken Books, 1972), 17–18.

2   Lon Milo DuQuette, *The Chicken Qabalah of Rabbi Lamed Ben Clifford: A Dilettante's Guide to What You Do and* Do Not *Need to Know to Become a Qabalist* (York Beach, ME: Red Wheel/Weiser, LLC, 2001).

3   April 12, 2017.

Introduction

1   DuQuette, *The Chicken Qabalah of Rabbi Lamed Ben Clifford: A Dilettante's Guide to What You Do and* Do Not *Need to Know to Become a Qabalist.* (York Beach, ME: Red Wheel/Weiser, LLC, 2001). [[AU: If we use endnotes rather than footnotes, we can treat this one with a shortened note form because the full entry appears above.]]

2   See *The Chicken Qabalah* for more biographical information.

3   Or so, until recently, it was assumed.

4   It would be a profound understatement to say *Son of Chicken Qabalah* would also not have materialized without Dr. Ben Lamed's selfless assistance.

5   It is perhaps worthy of note to point out that no financial paperwork— no bills, invoices, receipts, checkbook records, or bank statements— was found among the rabbi's effects. It appears that the O∴H∴O∴ collected no dues and charged no fees to its members. In fact, no membership records whatsoever were kept.

Qabalah Initiation: The Method to the Madness

1   *Brookhaven Locker Mss. no. 17* (folder labeled *"misc. correspondence with students who are smarter than I"*).

2   *Sephiroth,* plural; *Sephirah,* singular.

3   See *Chicken Qabalah,* 43.

4   Or *Sepher Yezirah.* See Appendices for required reading list.

5   *Chicken Qabalah,* 27–36.

6   *Chicken Qabalah,* 30.

7   The tuning fork essay was found in an envelope taped to the 1967 *Minimoog* synthesizer found among the rabbi's effects. It was obviously intended for the edification of the musician who plays an important role in the rabbi's initiation ceremonies.

8   Ninety days as a First-Degree, ninety days as a Second-Degree, and ninety days as a Third-Degree.

The Degree Ceremonies: Introductory Words

1   Ben Clifford disliked the word *psyche,* believing it too vague. He used it on occasion when it generally served the purpose. A more correct word in this instance might be *Neshamah*—the Soul Intuition: The third and second highest of the four parts of the Soul; corresponds to the first Heh (ה) [Heb: Heh]of the Tetragrammaton. See *Chicken Qabalah,* p. 99.

2   *Ruach*—the Intellect: The second of the four parts of the Soul; corresponds to Vav (ו) [Heb: Vav]of the Tetragrammaton. See *Chicken Qabalah,* p. 98.

3   It is a well-known fact that even though Ben Clifford was adept in his mastery of the Qabalistic applications of the Hebrew alphabet and key words, he was not fluent in the Hebrew language.

4 *The Book of the Coming Forth by Day.* In numerous editions. Based on the Papyrus of Ani, a Nineteenth Dynasty funerary text that guides the journey of the recently deceased through the various levels of consciousness, from layers of the death coma all the way to godhead.

5 *I.e.,* the dynamics of the three classes of letters of the Hebrew alphabet.

6 However, it appears that on one occasion adjustments were made to accommodate as many as twelve candidates during a single weekend marathon. A note (in the rabbi's hand) on the cover page of a specially annotated Third-Degree Script simply said, "I'll never ever ever ever ever ever ever do twelve at a time again .... EVER!"

First Degree: Preliminary Notes

1 A duplicate script written for male Candidates was also found in the rabbi's effects. A separate script annotated especially for the Musician was also found, giving more technical and detailed suggestions for the music and projector cues. This script, however, provides more than adequate instructions in footnotes.

Ceremony of Initiation: First-Degree

1 The waiting area for the First-Degree is a simple room adjacent to (or very near) the Temple room. There should be a comfortable chair for each candidate and a coffee table with cool water and light snacks. There should also be a small table supporting a mirror and a single white candle.

2 Editor's note: In this place in the initiation script, when WG makes reference to directions (East/West/North/South), she or he is not referring to geographic directions (or Temple directions as indicated by the small compass on the illustration of the Temple). Obviously, at the initial stages of creation (which the WG is enacting with these gestures), there is as yet no dimension of space, so the concept of geographic directions has no meaning. "Right/Left/Front/Back" would be just as descriptive.

3 See "Preliminary Notes" above for First-Degree Sign, Grip, and Word.

4 If the Candidate happens to answer "No" to this question, WG shall repeat the question slowly and clearly. If the Candidate again answers "No," WG shall remove him or her from the Temple and firmly, yet courteously, inform the Candidate that he or she must immediately leave the building and may not reapply for initiation for a period of one year. This is the standard practice whenever a Candidate refuses to respond in such a manner as to allow the ceremony to continue.

5   The Candidate and officers remain unshod whenever in the Temple room.

6   Jah, spelled Yod Heh (יה) [Heb: Heh Yod].

7   See note above.

8   *"Hell, yes (or Hell, no)! Don't worry about it!"* is one of several classic affirmations of *Chicken Qabalah*.

9   See *Chicken Qabalah*, Chapter 2, *The Ten Command-Rants*, 15–24:

1. All is One.

2. The First Command-Rant is a lie. All is Nothing.

3. There really isn't a creation, time or space, heaven or earth . . . but there is a you!

4. We perceive there is a creation, time and space, heaven and earth, because of a fundamental defect in our powers of perception.

5. This defect cannot be repaired, but it can be overcome.

6. In order to overcome our defective powers of perception we must be willing to abuse them until they break.

7. Everything in heaven and earth is connected to everything in heaven and earth.

8. Everything in heaven and earth is the reflection of everything in heaven and earth.

9. Everything in heaven and earth contains the pattern of everything in heaven and earth.

10. Look hard enough at anything and you will eventually see everything.

10 Editor's note: Marginal notes to the ritual script (and catering receipts found in the rabbi's records) suggest that an elaborately organized "evening meal and entertainment" were an integral and important part of the initiation ceremony itself. It was clear Ben Clifford wanted the Candidates to thoroughly enjoy themselves with food, wine, music, and laughter. It was also clear that he wanted the Candidates to have sufficient time after dinner to "sleep off" the effects of the festivities before bathing and returning for the midnight meditation and conclusion of the initiation.

11 Ideally, the scale range of the instrument should be from extremely low (e.g., the bass pedal notes of a pipe organ) to extremely high (*e.g.,*

high-frequency electronic tone). If this cannot be arranged, notes played on an organ, a harmonium, a piano, handbells, or a guitar will suffice. The only requirement is that several sustained notes creating specific musical notes and chords must be possible.

Editor's note: A choirmaster's pitch pipe was found among the rabbi's degree papers, suggesting that for at least one initiation ceremony he intoned the notes himself or enlisted the services of singers to create the musical effect cues.

12 Editor's note: The slide numbers appear to be irrelevant to anyone but the Musician/Technician. The extant copies of the script were unclear in spots, so we've simply left a question mark in place of a number.

13 A is the primal vibratory note attributed to the Hebrew letter *Tav* in its role as the primal dimensionless singularity of pre-creation and the primal center of dimensional creation.

14 E is the note associated with the Hebrew letter *Aleph*.

15 Note concerning the optical effect of the polarized or "flashing" colors: Although the phenomenon of the floating "ghost image" of the Hebrew letter is easy to produce on a brightly lit screen, the Candidates at first may need to be trained to see and hold the image in their mind's eye after they reclose their eyes. It may be necessary (especially for the first few tries) for the Officers (and Musician) to cycle through the series of slides several times until the Candidates excitedly indicate they "see" it.

16 For some people, the phenomenon of the floating ghost image is subtle and not immediately recognized (at least for the first few experiments). HT and WG should assure themselves that the Candidate is clearly recognizing the flashing color event before continuing with the next letter.

17 C is the note associated with the Hebrew letter *Shin*.

18 The Closing ceremony of each degree is a modified reversal of the Temple Opening (which the Candidates do not see). It is important that the newly initiated Candidates witness and take part in the Closing ceremonies so they may fully appreciate the formulae of the Letters the degree exemplifies.

First-Degree Study Program

1 See Appendix I for a partial list of works the rabbi expected every initiate to own. The list has been slightly updated by the editors to include valuable texts that have become available since the rabbi's disappearance.

2   In correspondence and essays, the rabbi inconsistently used the spelling *Sepher Yetzirah*. However, when making reference to a specific edition (as in this case), he used the particular spelling of the title *Sepher Yezirah* used by the publisher.

3   In contrast to traditions of other initiatory societies of the past (who tried to maintain a strict code of secrecy concerning their sacred ceremonies), it appears that the rabbi was happy to freely disseminate texts of the ceremonies without any mention of secrecy whatsoever.

4   P. 17 of this book.

5   Editor's note: Unfortunately, costs prohibit the publisher from including a pitch pipe with this book. Inexpensive quality pitch pipes are available at music stores (and, of course, on the internet).

6   The self-applied *Touch of Awakening*: right thumb on one's own right eyelid; right middle finger on left eyelid; right forefinger on center of forehead (third eye).

7   Dawn? Let's not kid ourselves. Few of us can arrange our lives to be able to do this regularly at dawn. The important thing is to take a few minutes *every day* (after you awaken and before you leave for work, school, or whatever occupies your day).

8   Always first cleanse your lungs with three *cleansing breaths* prior to any and every breathing exercise. (Inhale a deep, deep breath through the nose and hold for just a moment. Then exhale forcibly through the mouth, deeply emptying the lungs.)

9   The rabbi disliked the term *Astral Projection* and used it in this place only because it was a term familiar to most students that generally expressed this variety of psychic phenomenon. Ceremonial magicians of the Hermetic Order of the Golden Dawn called the exercise "Rising on the Planes" and "Traveling in the Spirit Vision."

10   Ben Clifford scrawled this note (in place of a tip) on the back of the check at Ms. Carolyn Tillie's *Qabalah Dinner House*, San Pedro.

11   The rabbi also disliked the term *Psychic Body* but would occasionally use it when it more or less served his purposes.

12   Sometimes spelled *scrying*.

13   *Pylon* in Egyptian, the *Egyptian Book of the Dead*.

14   A mild hallucination. The image may move or vibrate a bit.

15 The First-Degree *Sign* is a self-applied *Touch of Awakening*: right thumb on one's own right eyelid; right middle finger on left eyelid; right forefinger on center of forehead (third eye).

Second-Degree: Preliminary Notes

1 A duplicate script written for female Candidates was also found among the rabbi's papers. A separate script annotated especially for the Musician was also found, giving more technical and detailed suggestions for the music and projector cues. This script, however, provides more than adequate instructions in footnotes.

2 See First-Degree script, p. 21 of this book.

3 The waiting area for this degree is a small room furnished only with a chair positioned in front of a small table, which supports a dressing mirror and one white candle that provides the only light in the room. The only other objects on the table are the three-colored pipe cleaner "toy" from the First-Degree and the Candidate's own journal and a pen.

Ceremony of Initiation: Second-Degree

1 A large, artfully painted oilcloth (nearly 8 by 7 feet) was found rolled up among the rabbi's storage locker treasures.

2 Instructions on how temporary floorcloth designs can be created using colored masking tape were found among the rabbi's papers.

3 *Sepher Yezirah*, Chapter VI, Section 7.

4 In the script, music cues are centered and boxed.

5 A is the vibratory pitch of the letter *Tav*. At the word *Light*, Musician plays and holds the lowest A note possible—dramatically loud at first, but soon dropping lower and lower in volume until it becomes an almost inaudible hum. This low A is played whenever the Candidate is at the center and held until he steps off the center.

6 See First-Degree Initiation Ceremony, Part II.

7 As Candidate begins to walk, Musician plays and holds a middle-range E note for *Aleph*)—audible, but not intrusively loud.

8 As Candidate lights the candle, Musician plays a high-range E note (for *Beth*)—staccato, like the chiming of a bell.

9 As Candidate begins to walk, Musician plays and holds a middle-range E note (for *Aleph*)—audible, but not intrusively loud.

10 When Candidate reaches the Center, Musician again plays the lowest A note possible (for *Tav*)—holding it for only a moment.

11 As Candidate begins to walk, Musician again plays and holds a middle-range E note (for *Aleph*)—audible, but not intrusively loud.

12 G# is the vibratory pitch of the letter *Gimel*. As Candidate lights the candle, Musician plays and holds a high-range G# note—staccato, like the chiming of a bell.

13 As Candidate begins to walk, Musician again plays and holds a middle-range E note (for *Aleph*)—audible, but not intrusively loud.

14 When Candidate reaches the center, Musician again plays the lowest A note possible (for *Tav*)—holding it for only a moment.

15 G# is also the vibratory pitch for the letter *Mem*. As Candidate begins to walk, Musician plays and holds a middle-range G# note (for *Mem*)—audible, but not intrusively loud.

16 F# is the vibratory pitch of the letter *Daleth*. As Candidate lights the candle, Musician plays and holds a high-range F# note (for *Daleth*)—staccato, like the chiming of a bell.

17 As Candidate begins to walk, Musician plays and holds a middle-range G# note (for *Mem*)—audible, but not intrusively loud.

18 When Candidate reaches the center, Musician again plays the lowest A note possible (for *Tav*)—holding it for only a moment.

19 As Candidate begins to walk, Musician again plays and holds a middle-range G# note (for *Mem*)—audible, but not intrusively loud.

20 B♭ is the vibratory pitch of the letter *Kaph*. As Candidate lights the candle, Musician plays and holds a high-range B♭ note (for *Kaph*)—staccato, like the chiming of a bell.

21 As Candidate begins to walk, Musician again plays and holds a middle-range G# note (for *Mem*)—audible, but not intrusively loud.

22 When Candidate reaches the center, Musician again plays the lowest A note possible (for *Tav*)—holding it for only a moment.

23 C is the vibratory pitch of the letter *Shin*. As Candidate begins to walk, Musician plays and holds a middle-range C note (for *Shin*)—audible, but not intrusively loud.

24 C is also the vibratory pitch of the letter *Peh*. This C, however, is played at the highest octave possible—staccato, like the chiming of a bell.

25 As Candidate begins to walk, Musician plays and holds a middle-range C note (for *Shin*)—audible, but not intrusively loud.

26 When Candidate reaches the center, Musician again plays the lowest A note possible (for *Tav*)—holding it for only a moment.

27 As Candidate begins to walk, Musician plays and holds a middle-range C note (for *Shin*)—audible, but not intrusively loud.

28 D is the vibratory pitch of the letter *Resh*. As Candidate lights the candle, Musician plays and holds a high-range D note (for *Resh*)—staccato, like the chiming of a bell.

29 As Candidate begins to walk, Musician plays and holds a middle-range C note (for *Shin*)—audible, but not intrusively loud.

30 When Candidate reaches the center, Musician again plays the lowest A note possible (for *Tav*)—holding it for only a moment.

31 In this version of the script, the music and image cues are centered in the page and enclosed in a box.

32 Editor's note: The slide numbers appear to be irrelevant to anyone but the Musician/Technician. The extant copies of the script were unclear in spots, so we've simply left a question mark in place of a number.

33 *Sepher Yezirah*, Chapter VI, Section 7.

Second-Degree: Study Program

1 Because the extension of the primal Three Mother Letters initiates the subsequent sequence of events that create the Double and Simple Letters, the First-Degree Sign and Word serve as the master key to enter new levels of consciousness. The First-Degree Sign is a self-applied *Touch of Awakening*: right thumb on one's own right eyelid; right middle finger on left eyelid; right forefinger on center of forehead (third eye).

Third-Degree: Preliminary Notes

1 A duplicate script written for male Candidates was also found among the rabbi's papers. A separate script annotated especially for the Musician was also found, giving more technical and detailed suggestions for the music and projector cues. This script, however, provides more than adequate instructions in footnotes.

2 In fact, a Canadian Army first-aid kit was found among the rabbi's effects.

3 See p. 21.

4   See p. 81.

5   HT's chair remains in place, and it is not necessary to lay out the Second-Degree floorcloth for this brief Second-Degree Opening.

6   A box of extra-long wooden fireplace matches was found among the rabbi's effects.

7   The waiting area for this degree is the same as for the Second-Degree—a small room furnished only with a chair positioned in front of a small table that supports a dressing mirror and one white candle that provides the only light in the room. The only other objects on the table are the Candidate's own journal and a pen, the three-colored pipe cleaner "toy" from the First-Degree, and a new "Third-Degree Cube toy" (see Figure 17). This cube is an amended version of the Second-Degree toy but with the Twelve Simple Letters and zodiac symbols added to the twelve edges. Also lying on the table is a single long-stemmed red rose. The stem should still be covered with sharp thorns. (Editor's note: After the ceremony is concluded, both the rose and the cube are given to the new initiate as souvenirs.)

Ceremony of Initiation: Third-Degree

1   A large, artfully painted oilcloth (nearly 8 by 7 feet) was found rolled up among the storage locker treasures.

2   James Thomson, *The City of Dreadful Night*. Originally published in *The National Reformer*, 1874.

3   A small *Musician's Manual* was found among the rabbi's effects. However, the directions that appear within the initiation scripts are clear and more than adequate to the purposes of this work.

4   Editor's note: The slide numbers appear to be irrelevant to anyone but the Musician/Technician. The extant copies of the script were unclear in spots, so we've simply left a question mark in place of a number.

5   See "Third-Degree Study Materials" for description and form for the Dodecahedron.

6   *Sepher Yezirah*, Chapter I, section 1.

7   See Appendix II.

8   All vowels chanted for this exercise are the initial letter sound followed by an extended open-mouth "ahhhhhhhh."

Third-Degree: Study Program

1   Editor's note: See Chapter Ten of *Chicken Qabalah*, "Rabbi Lamed Ben Clifford's Last Lecture: Games Qabalists Play," 179.

2   Editor's note: For the exercises that follow in this section, it is essential that the reader have at hand a copy of *The Chicken Qabalah* and other reference texts such as *777*.

3   Because the extension of the primal Three Mother Letters initiates the subsequent sequence of events that create the Double and Simple Letters, the First-Degree Sign and Word serve as the master key to enter new levels of consciousness. The First-Degree Sign is a self-applied *Touch of Awakening*: right thumb on one's own right eyelid; right middle finger on left eyelid; right forefinger on center of forehead (third eye).

Epilogue

1   From an undated and unsent letter to Mel Brooks.

Appendix I: Chicken Qabalist's Reference Library

1   Amended slightly by the editor to include pertinent works made available after the rabbi's disappearance.

Appendix II: The Thirty-Two Paths of Wisdom

1   From the Hebrew Text of Joannes Stephanus Rittangelius (1642). Translation by William Wynn Westcott (1877).

ABOUT THE AUTHOR

In the dark and brooding firmament of occult literature, Lon Milo DuQuette is a star of unique and exceptional brilliance who has earned the distinction of being able to make complex magical and spiritual concepts amusing, entertaining, and easily digestible. This rare combination of scholarship and self-effacing humor has in the last thirty years secured him a unique and respected position in the world of esoteric literature. He is an internationally recognized authority on Ceremonial Magick, Qabalah, Tarot, and the life and teachings of noted English occultist Aleister Crowley (1875–1947). DuQuette has authored seventeen books (translated into twelve languages), including *The Chicken Qabalah of Rabbi Lamed Ben Clifford* and *Understanding Aleister Crowley's Thoth Tarot*. His passion for writing is not limited to his magick. He is also an award-winning singer-songwriter and recording artist whose musical career has spanned over fifty years.

Since 1975, DuQuette has served as an administrative officer of *Ordo Templi Orientis* (O.T.O.), one of the most influential and controversial magical societies of the 20th (now 21st) century. He is an acknowledged authority on the life and works of Aleister Crowley (the 100-year-old organization's most celebrated and notorious leader). Since 1994, he has served as the O.T.O.'s United States Deputy National Grand Master. He travels extensively each year to lecture, teach, and perform his music. He is arguably the Order's most visible representative.

Born in Long Beach, California, in 1948, he moved as a child to Columbus, Nebraska, where he would meet his wife-to-be, Constance (his high-school sweetheart). Moving back to California the moment he graduated from high school, Lon promptly proposed to Constance over the telephone (under the mystical inspiration of LSD). They were married in 1967 and have remained magickal partners ever since. (This is an accomplishment Lon considers his greatest magical achievement.) They have one son, Dr. Jean-Paul DuQuette of Macau, China.

To Our Readers

Weiser Books, an imprint of Red Wheel/Weiser, publishes books across the entire spectrum of occult, esoteric, speculative, and New Age subjects. Our mission is to publish quality books that will make a difference in people's lives without advocating any one particular path or field of study. We value the integrity, originality, and depth of knowledge of our authors.

Our readers are our most important resource, and we appreciate your input, suggestions, and ideas about what you would like to see published.

Visit our website at *www.redwheelweiser.com* to learn about our upcoming books and free downloads, and be sure to go to *www.redwheelweiser.com/ newsletter* to sign up for newsletters and exclusive offers.

You can also contact us at *info@rwwbooks.com* or at

Red Wheel/Weiser, LLC
65 Parker Street, Suite 7
Newburyport, MA 01950